OECD Multi-level Governance Studies

Strengthening Place-Based Regional Development Policy in Estonia

OECD
BETTER POLICIES FOR BETTER LIVES

Please cite this publication as:
OECD (2025), *Strengthening Place-Based Regional Development Policy in Estonia*, OECD Multi-level Governance Studies, OECD Publishing, Paris, https://doi.org/10.1787/45e0cdc7-en.

ISBN 978-92-64-70647-7 (print)
ISBN 978-92-64-54472-7 (PDF)
ISBN 978-92-64-91850-4 (HTML)

OECD Multi-level Governance Studies
ISSN 2414-6781 (print)
ISSN 2414-679X (online)

Photo credits: Cover © NordicMoonlight / Getty Images Plus.

Corrigenda to OECD publications may be found at: https://www.oecd.org/en/publications/support/corrigenda.html.

Foreword

Pointing to a striking difference in economic output between the capital region and others, the Estonian Government acknowledges regional inequality as a significant national challenge, and the need for a new approach to promote balanced growth and improve well-being across the territory. As a step in this direction, Estonia has introduced two pilot regional councils – one for South Estonia and one for Central Estonia – to identify and capitalise on the development potential of each region. These pilots also aim to strengthen the role of subnational governments in policy design and implementation, helping to ensure that regional perspectives are better reflected in national sectoral policies. Produced at the request of the Estonian Government and its Ministry of Finance, this report contributes to the government's efforts by reviewing Estonia's approach to improving multi-level governance for regional development, including through the pilot regional councils. This report is part of the European Commission-funded project Strengthening Regional Specialisation and Competitiveness in Estonia.

The report brings together findings from a number of activities undertaken between 2023 and 2025. First, futures and foresight workshops brought together a broad range of stakeholders from each of the pilot regions to consider what potential futures their region might face. These were followed by a set of vision-setting workshops to guide stakeholders through the process of defining desired futures. Action plan workshops were also leveraged to assist the two regional councils through a process of developing concrete roadmaps for achieving their regions' ambitions, which could, in turn, feed into regional development agreements. A capacity-building workshop for the councils focused on contracts and agreements among levels of government, bringing together experts from the OECD and the Icelandic Ministry of Infrastructure sharing Iceland's experiences. Finally, a workshop for vice-chancellors and senior officials from across the Estonian Government provided a platform to explore how better cross-ministry co-ordination can produce stronger outcomes for regions and sectors.

The experience of Estonia articulated by stakeholders in those fora and in this report echoes the messages of the OECD Recommendation on Regional Development Policy, including the importance of leveraging each region's specific competitive and absolute advantages, and strengthening multi-level governance to promote effective co-ordination among levels of government and across parts of government.

This report was undertaken as part of the programme of work of the OECD's Regional Development Policy Committee (RDPC), a leading international forum in the fields of regional, urban and rural development policy and multi-level governance, and delivered by the Centre for Entrepreneurship, SMEs, Regions and Cities (CFE). This report was submitted to the RDPC for comment on 3 June 2025 under cote CFE/RDPC(2025)8.

Acknowledgements

This report was produced by the OECD Centre for Entrepreneurship, SMEs, Regions and Cities (CFE), led by Lamia Kamal-Chaoui, Director, as part of the programme of work of the Regional Development Policy Committee (RDPC). The project was funded by the European Union via the Technical Support Instrument and implemented by the OECD, in co-operation with the European Commission.

The report was led and co-ordinated by Alexis Durand, under the supervision of Maria Varinia Michalun, Head of the Governance and Strategic Planning Unit in the Regional Development and Multi-level Governance Division of the CFE, led by Dorothée Allain-Dupré. The report was drafted by Alexis Durand, Maria Varinia Michalun and Yingyin Wu. The report also benefits from the inputs and review of Betty-Ann Bryce, David Burgalassi, Claire Charbit, Michael Flood, Janis Jurgeleit, Antti Moiso, Eduardo Montemayor, Atte Oksanen and Josh Wood (CFE). Albertína Friðbjörg Elíasdóttir (Association of Municipalities in Northeast Iceland), Hanna Dóra Hólm Másdóttir and Hólmfríður Sveinsdóttir (Icelandic Ministry of Infrastructure) shared their insight on Iceland's regional plans of action. Eric Reese facilitated one of the project workshops.

The OECD would like to thank the Estonian Government for its co-operation and support throughout this project. Special thanks are due to the Local Governments Policy Department of the Ministry of Regional Affairs and Agriculture and the ministry staff (past and present) that worked closely with the OECD and European Commission to bring this project to fruition; special thanks go to Rainer Eidemiller, Sigrid Soomlais, Mart Uusjärv, Sulev Valner and Ave Viks. Thanks are extended to the various ministries across the Estonian Government that participated in the focus groups and workshops.

Sincere thanks are given to the pilot regional councils in Central and South Estonia for their warm welcome and enthusiastic participation in the workshops with the OECD. We would also like to thank the large number of stakeholders from the private and third sector, academia and other fields who shared their time and perspectives with the OECD team.

Jack Waters (CFE) led the process of preparing the manuscript for publication, and Eleonore Morena copy-edited the report.

Table of contents

Foreword 3

Acknowledgements 4

Executive summary 8

1 A role for place-based policy for regional development in Estonia 10
- Introduction 11
- Reconsidering Estonia: From “one single territory” to “five regions, one nation” 12
- The differentiated economic performance of Estonia’s regions 16
- Enablers for regional well-being in Estonia’s regions 25
- Capitalising on regional differences: Different visions, different tools in Central and South Estonia 30
- Conclusion 35
- References 36
- Notes 43

2 Laying the foundations for place-based regional development in Estonia 45
- Introduction 46
- Driving a co-ordinated regional approach across the national government 47
- Empowering subnational actors to enable a place-based approach 57
- Conclusion 68
- References 69
- Notes 76

3 Experimenting with regional governance for a place-based approach to regional development 77
- Introduction 78
- The idea: Three drivers behind the pilot regional councils 80
- The implementation: The pilot regional councils in practice 84
- The results: The two pilot regional development agreements 92
- The future: Evaluating and learning from the experiment 96
- Conclusion 101
- References 102
- Notes 105

Annex A. Project methodology 106

Annex B. Additional figures 107

FIGURES

Figure 1.1. A large rural area, and varying access to cities across Estonian regions 13
Figure 1.2. Apart from the capital region, Estonian regions are expected to shrink 14
Figure 1.3. Net migration – both internal and external – is highest in the capital region 16
Figure 1.4. Estonia's economy is experiencing a relatively severe downturn 19
Figure 1.5. Regional disparities in labour productivity persist, despite improvements in non-capital regions 21
Figure 1.6. Northeast Estonia has a considerably lower employment rate than the other regions 23
Figure 1.7. Educational attainment by region 28
Figure 3.1. A trio of motivations for establishing the regional councils 80

Figure A B.1. Net internal migration 107
Figure A B.2. Net external migration 108
Figure A B.3. Value-added by region and sector 109
Figure A B.4. Labour productivity in agriculture, forestry and fishing, 2013-22 111
Figure A B.5. Labour productivity in industry (except construction), 2013-22 111
Figure A B.6. Labour productivity in manufacturing, 2013-22 112
Figure A B.7. Labour productivity in construction, 2013-22 112
Figure A B.8. Labour productivity in wholesale and retail trade, repair of motor vehicles and motorcycles, transportation and storage, accommodation and food service activities, 2013-22 113
Figure A B.9. Labour productivity in information and communication, 2013-22 113
Figure A B.10. Labour productivity in financial and insurance activities, 2013-22 114
Figure A B.11. Labour productivity in real estate activities, 2013-22 114
Figure A B.12. Labour productivity in professional, scientific and technical activities, administrative and support service activities, 2013-22 115
Figure A B.13. Labour productivity in public administration, defence, education, human health and social work activities, 2013-22 115
Figure A B.14. Labour productivity in arts, entertainment and recreation, other service activities, activities of household and extraterritorial organisations and bodies, 2013-22 116
Figure A B.15. Pre-primary, primary and lower secondary educational attainment 116
Figure A B.16. Upper secondary and post-secondary non-tertiary educational attainment 117
Figure A B.17. Tertiary educational attainment 117

TABLES

Table 1.1. Classification of the five Estonian TL3 regions 12
Table 1.2. Estonia's regions have different drivers of economic growth 17
Table 1.3. Economic indicators of Estonia's regions 20
Table 1.4. Development ambitions in Central and South Estonia 31
Table 2.1. Three missing prerequisites for place-based policy for regional development 46
Table 2.2. Estonia 2035 frames sectoral activities as primary contributors to regional development goals 49
Table 2.3. Estonian local authorities manage a significant share of competences, many of which are shared with the national government 60
Table 3.1. Advantages and risks of proposed governance models 79
Table 3.2. A range of regional governance models in OECD countries 81
Table 3.3. Planned and actual members of the pilot regional councils 86
Table 3.4. Examples of qualitative and quantitative measures that could help evaluate the experiment of the pilot regional councils 99

Table A B.1. Value-added by region, sector, and subsector, 2023 109

BOXES

Box 1.1. *Shrinking Smartly in Estonia* 15
Box 1.2. How has the Estonian economy performed overall? 19
Box 1.3. Policies for rural productivity 22
Box 1.4. Place-based labour and skills policies: Neighbourhood employment support policies 24
Box 2.1. A brief history of regional development policy in Estonia 48
Box 2.2. Regional development and Estonia's Rules for Good Legislative and Regulatory Process 50
Box 2.3. Northern Ireland in the United Kingdom promotes high-quality assessment of policy impact on rural areas 52
Box 2.4. A co-ordination platform for the political and operational sides of regional development in Sweden 54
Box 2.5. Creating a financial incentive to work together to implement Italy's National Strategy for Inner Areas 56
Box 2.6. Territorial administrative reforms in Estonia 59
Box 2.7. A digital platform to support municipal planning in Czechia 63
Box 2.8. Tools to ensure strategic coherence across levels of government in Czechia and Poland 65
Box 2.9. National-local co-financing as a way to ensure strategic alignment among levels of government 66
Box 3.1. The birth of an idea: A recognition that regional governance could be a tool to promote balanced growth 79
Box 3.2. Inter-municipal co-operation in Estonia is rare, despite the benefits it could offer to small and shrinking municipalities 82
Box 3.3. Regional Plans of Action show their value as a tool for engagement with municipalities in Iceland 87
Box 3.4. The stages of the contractual process 89
Box 3.5. Transactional versus relational contracts 90
Box 3.6. Mutual, credible commitments are the backbone of agreements among levels of government 93
Box 3.7. The ABCDs of policy experimentation for regional development 97
Box 3.8. An iterative, experimental approach to regionalisation in Sweden 100

Executive summary

Estonia's starkest regional disparity is that between the capital region and other regions. The capital region – North Estonia – is home to nearly half of the population, generates over 60% of national gross domestic product and outperforms other regions across most economic and labour market indicators. Its labour productivity is 53% higher than that of the least productive region (West Estonia). Population trends mirror these divides: while North Estonia continues to grow, the country has shrunk by 15% since 1991, with projections of further shrinking upwards of 15% in some regions by 2050. These patterns are accompanied and influenced by gaps in regional health outcomes, educational outcomes and transport connectivity, particularly outside the main urban hubs. Each region is characterised by a different mix of sector specialisations, from oil shale in Northeast Estonia, to agriculture in Central Estonia, the university and innovation base of South Estonia and the tourism economy of West Estonia.

Recognising Estonia's territorial differences is the starting point for each region's development potential. While the national objectives of economic growth and well-being may be shared among all regions, how they contribute to meeting these objectives vary depending on the challenges each region faces, the assets they have and the ambitions they hold. Place-based policy for regional development can align national action with these distinct assets and ambitions, helping regions to address disadvantages and realise their potential. In Estonia, like other countries, this calls for policy tools that are sensitive to the needs, opportunities and characteristics of different regions.

Key findings and recommendations

Estonia's national policies remain largely spatially blind. While Estonia's national strategy (Estonia 2035) contains a target to reduce regional disparities, line ministries generally pursue national objectives with limited regard for their potential asymmetric or differential impacts in regions. In doing so, however, national policy can inadvertently prioritise development in urban areas, as evidenced by the urban concentration of funding for business support and infrastructure. Estonia lacks some governance tools that could promote a stronger place-based approach to regional development, such as a regional development policy or structures for cross-government collaboration that systematically embody regional development challenges or goals. Ministries' assessment of regional impact – required when introducing new laws and policies – is sometimes perfunctory. To help make national policy more responsive to regional development needs and opportunities, Estonia is encouraged to:

- Expand the use of explicit agreements for ministries to work together for regional development. The Ministry of Regional Affairs and Agriculture could enter into contracts with other ministries to formalise how they will work towards complementary goals, particularly those contributing to regional development (including goals in the Central and South Estonian regional development agreements).
- Strengthen regional impact assessment. This may entail providing specific training and guidance for line ministries on assessments and introducing accountability mechanisms such as a public "regional impact dashboard" showing expected regional impact of new laws and strategies.

- Create space for regular cross-ministerial dialogue on regional development. This could include dedicated sessions for ministers within the Economic Cabinet and a civil-servant-level steering committee focused on regional development to "connect the dots" across sectors.

Subnational actors sometimes lack the necessary financial and strategic capacity that would better support a place-based approach. Own-source revenue of Estonian municipalities is among the lowest of OECD countries, which limits their ability to spend or invest in areas beyond their core tasks. This context helps to explain why the county plans they negotiate occasionally end up listing projects they hope will receive national funding. Exacerbating this tendency are weak connections between national and local governments on regional development, without strong mechanisms to find opportunities for collaboration. With low own-source revenue and a strong prevalence of earmarked grants (81% of grants from the national government), municipalities tend to fill the role of service providers rather than active partners in shaping their regions' development. To strengthen the capacity of subnational governments to respond to regional challenges and build regional competitiveness, Estonia is encouraged to:

- Help municipalities and county development organisations develop strong strategic plans, for example by updating national guidance on county planning to encourage the use of vision setting, scenario planning and prioritisation. This guidance can be supported with a dedicated online hub offering training, templates and examples of good practice.
- Harness national and subnational strategic planning processes to find new opportunities for activities to be complementary and mutually enforcing. One way to support this is by expanding the national strategy platform that lists all national strategies to include county development strategies, and mapping how local, county and national objectives interconnect.

The Central and South Estonian pilot regional councils represent a significant step towards policy that is more responsive to the needs and opportunities of the two regions. The councils bring together national ministries, local governments and regional stakeholders to create regional development agreements that define regional priorities, and the activities suggested to realise them. In doing so, the councils have created a new space for shared priority setting, co-ordination and collaboration. To build on this step towards place-based policy for regional development, Estonia is encouraged to:

- Broaden national government participation in future regional councils, including by targeting ministries that did not participate in the pilots (e.g. environment, social affairs) by demonstrating shared benefits and coherence across policy spaces.
- Make a clear distinction for future regional councils between an initial scoping phase, where council members consult with stakeholders to identify regional challenges and opportunities, and a later negotiation phase, where councils negotiate a final agreement among signatories.
- Ensure that future regional development agreements are credible by clarifying who is doing what and with what resources to implement the agreements. Commitments should be accompanied by provisions for monitoring and enforcement to ensure that parties adhere to their commitments.
- Conduct an evaluation of the pilot regional councils to assess whether they have met objectives, using quantitative and qualitative measures and involving a broad range of stakeholders. Making the evaluation independent can help to ensure it is objective.

1 A role for place-based policy for regional development in Estonia

This chapter focuses on the distinct regional development needs and opportunities of Estonia's regions. It analyses how current patterns of urbanisation, population and economic activity differ across Estonia's regions and identifies gaps in economic, labour market and well-being outcomes. Recognising that place-based policies can target not only regional disadvantages but also regional assets and ambitions, the chapter also considers the unique strengths and development goals of Estonia's two pilot regional councils in Central and South Estonia. It highlights opportunities for how national policy can better respond to regional contexts. This includes recognising regional assets and opportunities and aligning tools and resources to support them. In doing so, this chapter makes the case for how a more place-based approach can strengthen Estonia's regional development efforts.

Introduction

Estonian regions have different needs, assets and ambitions for development. In Estonia, headlines about regional inequality often focus on the stark contrast between the capital region and the rest of the country (e.g. "Tallinn continues to account for more than half of Estonia's GDP" (ERR, 2024[1])). Certainly, the capital region plays an outsized role in the country's economy and tends to perform better in major indicators of health and education. Remove this hub from national statistics and the scale of difference among the remaining regions is less dramatic. Even among non-capital regions, however, distinct development patterns and priorities emerge. A closer look at both data and testimony from residents reveal that Estonia's regions have their own distinct needs, assets and ambitions that can be addressed and harnessed for regional development. These distinct features began to take shape in the European Union-funded OECD project with the Estonian Government - Strengthening Regional Competitiveness and Specialisation (Annex A) - which covered 2 regions, together encompassing 9 of Estonia's 15 counties.

Taking a place-based approach in Estonia will mean recognising and responding to the diverse conditions and opportunities of Estonia's regions, beyond the binary of Tallinn versus the rest of the country. Over time, place-based policy for regional development has evolved from a focus on less-developed regions towards place-sensitivity encompassing all regions. It increasingly takes a more proactive approach, helping regions navigate shifts in industry or demographics for example (Suedekum, 2023[2]). Central to this approach is the national government's development of a deep understanding of local context, acting on and responding to the conditions and opportunities of a given place (OECD, 2025[3]). In Estonia, this means that a place-based approach should not just aim to address regional disadvantages but also build on the distinct regional assets and ambitions of all Estonian regions.

This section begins by exploring differences in major demographic, economic and well-being indicators among Estonian regions. It describes patterns of settlement and urbanisation across regions, showing how population and urbanisation are concentrated in one large urban hub (centred around Tallinn) and two smaller cities (Narva and Tartu), while the rest of the country is predominantly rural and sparsely populated. The section then explores differences in the economic bases of each region, showing how each region relies on different mixes of agriculture, industry and services. It shows that labour market outcomes across regions are uneven, with the capital region outperforming other regions. Finally, the section identifies disparities in health, education and connectivity, shaped in part by differences in access to services. This report uses small, Territorial Level 3 (TL3) regions[1] as the scale of its analysis.

The final part of this chapter shows that Estonia's regions differ not only in their development profiles but also in their assets and ambitions for development. It focuses on Central and South Estonia, the two regions that participated as pilots in the Estonian Government's experiment with regional councils as a means to foster a more place-based approach to development. These regions participated in interviews and focus groups with the OECD, sharing their perspectives on regional assets and ambitions. For example, participants in South Estonia wanted to build on the region's proximity to Tartu's universities to drive innovation and knowledge-based growth. Participants in Central Estonia, meanwhile, wanted to leverage its strong vocational education system and cultural heritage to position the region as a family-friendly place for entrepreneurs and workers. In parallel, each region was developing a formal expression of their development ambitions through the process of negotiating and drafting regional development agreements (Chapter 3). These two regions are examples of how different combinations of assets can be leveraged – including through place-based policy – to support regional development that reflects each region's unique context and potential.

Reconsidering Estonia: From "one single territory" to "five regions, one nation"

Despite its relatively small territorial and population size, Estonia's regions have different urbanisation or population patterns, which in turn have a differentiated effect on their development. These differences are reflected in their TL3 classifications, which show how regions differ in their access to functional urban areas (FUAs) and their rural or urban makeup (Table 1.1). These territorial distinctions provide context for understanding the regional development challenges Estonian regions face – particularly in economic output, labour market outcomes and public service delivery. Policy makers should consider these differences when designing regional development interventions, be they sector-driven or cross-sector in nature. In addition, it is these differences – and how they are experienced on the ground – that lead regions, their enterprises and residents to seek development solutions tailored to their own distinct needs, assets and ambitions.

Table 1.1. Classification of the five Estonian TL3 regions

	Access to an FUA	Rural/urban
Central Estonia	Remote (NMR-R)	Predominantly rural, remote (PRR)
North Estonia	Metropolitan midsize (MR-M)	Predominantly urban (PU)
Northeast Estonia	Near a small FUA (NMR-S)	Predominantly urban (PU)
South Estonia	Near a small FUA (NMR-S)	Predominantly rural, close to a city (PRC)
West Estonia	Remote (NMR-R)	Predominantly rural, remote (PRR)

Source: OECD (n.d.[4]), *OECD Geographical Definitions*, https://www.oecd.org/en/data/datasets/oecd-geographical-definitions.html.

Urbanisation and population in Estonia

Patterns in urbanisation and population data help to explain why some regions face greater challenges in their development than others. Agglomeration – where people, businesses and activity concentrate in an area – shapes regional development by reinforcing productivity advantages in cities and places connected to cities. In short, agglomeration economies occur when "productivity rises with density" (Glaeser and Gottlieb, 2009[5]). Urban agglomerations – cities – tend to generate higher economic output not only because they attract more skilled workers but because they create productivity gains through mechanisms like knowledge spillovers, labour market matching and shared infrastructure (Ahrend et al., 2017[6]; Ahrend, Lembcke and Schumann, 2017[7]). This advantage grows as cities grow: labour productivity tends to increase with city size. In addition, the benefits spill into the regions that surround cities, which benefit from "borrowed size" (i.e. they capture some productivity benefits without being large themselves) (Ahrend, Lembcke and Schumann, 2017[7]). In general, as connections between cities and surrounding areas become thinner, however, these spillovers weaken (Marshalian, Chan and Bournisien de Valmont, 2023[8]). In Estonia, the concentration of people and economic activity in a small number of urban centres (discussed in the next section) provides economic advantages for these centres and their surroundings,[2] while large parts of the country that are remote and sparsely populated may not benefit from urban spillovers.

Estonia's regions differ in terms of their urbanisation and proximity to cities (Figure 1.1). The country includes one very urbanised region – North Estonia – centred around the capital city of Tallinn. This is the country's most urbanised and populous region. It forms the only major metropolitan FUA,[3] home to close to one-half of the national population (646 315 people) in 2024. South Estonia, anchored by the city of Tartu, contains a secondary though mid-sized urban hub, with a FUA of 164 460 inhabitants (OECD, 2024[9]). The large rural area surrounding Tartu and its FUA earn it a classification of "predominantly rural, close to a city" in the OECD Extended Regional Typology (Brezzi, Dijkstra and Ruiz, 2011[10]). Northeast Estonia contains the small city of Narva and its own small FUA (population of 53 360) (OECD, 2024[9]).

While Narva is relatively small in terms of population, the Northeast Estonia region is dense enough[4] to be classified as predominantly urban. The remaining regions – Central and West Estonia – are more rural and remote, lacking large cities and facing more limited access to urban centres (Fadic et al., 2019[11]).

Figure 1.1. A large rural area, and varying access to cities across Estonian regions

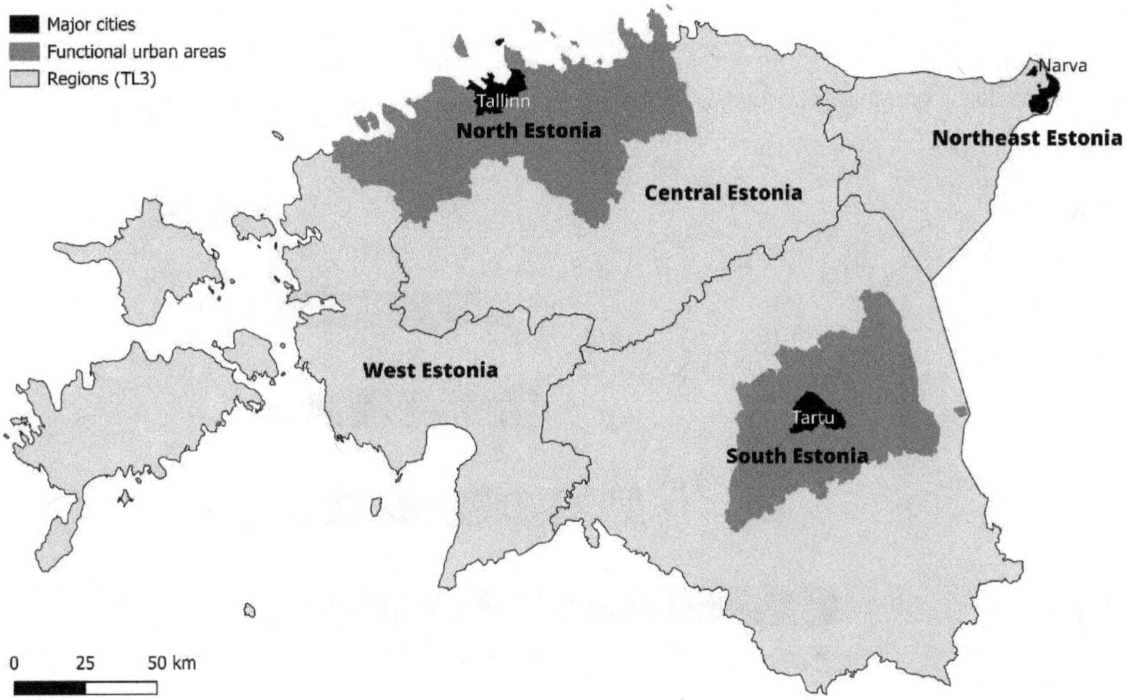

Source: OECD (n.d.[4]), *OECD Geographical Definitions*, https://www.oecd.org/en/data/datasets/oecd-geographical-definitions.html.

Estonia's population is concentrated in its two dominant urban centres but it also has a substantial rural population. Nearly 70% of Estonia's total population of close to 1.4 million lived in urban areas in 2023 (CIA, 2023[12]; Statistics Estonia, 2023[13]), with about a third residing in Tallinn alone. The next largest city – Tartu – accounted for a little more than 7% of the national population (Statistics Estonia, 2023[14]). Young people are also concentrated in Estonia's urban areas: 33% of the country's young people (aged 0-29) live in Tallinn, with Tartu accounting for an additional 8% (Statistics Estonia, 2024[15]). Despite the high – and highly concentrated – urban population, among OECD countries, Estonia has one of the highest shares of population living in non-metropolitan remote regions: 21%, compared to the OECD average of 8.1% (Fadic et al., 2019[11]). This reflects Estonia's unique territorial profile: while urban centres dominate demographically (and economically, as explored below), much of the country remains sparsely populated with residents that are geographically distant from these major urban hubs.

Except for the capital region, all of Estonia's regions face the challenge of a shrinking population. Estonia's total population has already shrunk by 15% since 1991 (OECD, 2022[16]). Recent years, however, have seen national population increasing slightly (close to 4% between 2014 and 2023), due largely to population increase in North Estonia (nearly 12% during this period). The population of other regions has either hovered around the same value or declined during this period, with the largest decline occurring in

Northeast Estonia (nearly 11%) (OECD, 2024[17]). There are exceptions within the regions: some counties within the four non-capital regions – notably Pärnu and Rapla counties in West and Central Estonia respectively – have experienced population growth (Estonian Ministry of Finance, 2021, p. 20[18]). Projections suggest further shrinking in non-capital regions: only one region is projected to continue growing – the capital region – while other regions are projected to lose upwards of 15% of their population by 2050 (Figure 1.2). A shrinking population has wide-ranging consequences for affected regions and Estonia's national government (Box 1.1), including increasing the cost of public service delivery and straining local budgets.

Figure 1.2. Apart from the capital region, Estonian regions are expected to shrink

Projected population growth by TL3 region, 2024-50

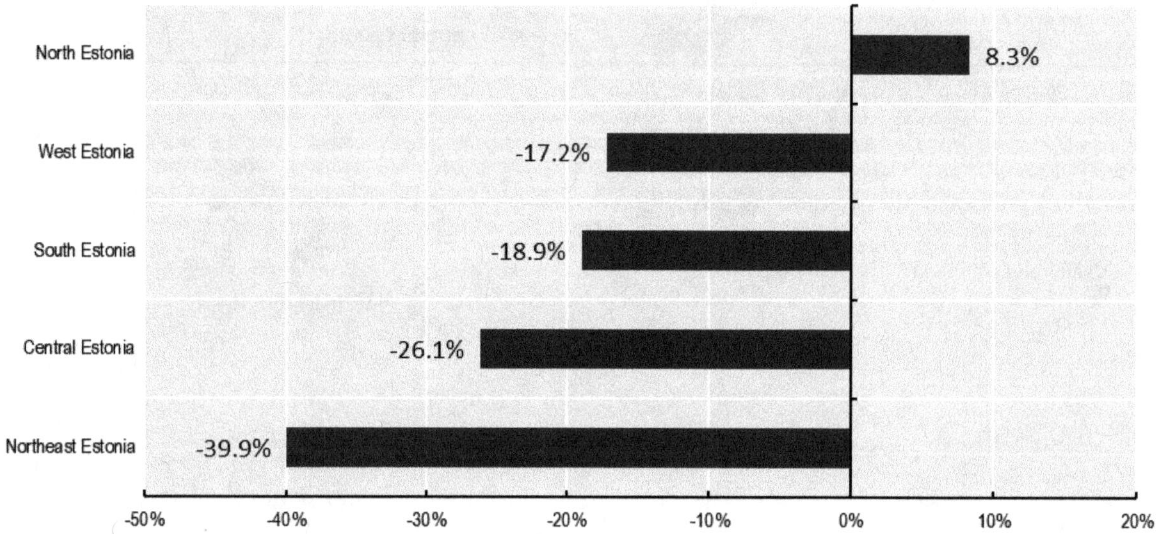

Source: Eurostat (2024[19]), *Population on 1st January by Age, Sex, Type of Projection and NUTS 3 Region*, https://ec.europa.eu/eurostat/databrowser/view/proj_19rp3$defaultview/default/table.

Box 1.1. *Shrinking Smartly in Estonia*

Population decline has far-reaching implications for regional economies, service provision and governance. As the report *Shrinking Smartly in Estonia: Preparing Regions for Demographic Change* highlights, shrinking populations in Estonia, particularly in rural and remote areas, lead to higher per capita costs for infrastructure and public services, such as education and healthcare, while simultaneously reducing municipal revenues (OECD, 2022[16]). It has a myriad of other impacts as well, including housing vacancies, deteriorating built environments and labour market shortages. Ultimately, these effects can reinforce regional disparities, making it harder for these regions to attract investment or retain young people.

In the report, the OECD provides recommendations for Estonian regions to prepare for a shrinking population. These include the following:

- The Estonian Government could do more to promote integrated and effective multi-level governance, overcoming fragmentation among levels of government and silos between policy areas on the national level. This includes providing fiscal transfers to inter-municipal bodies instead of municipalities.
- Municipalities have little financial independence, which weakens decision making and discourages discretionary decision making that can result in efficiency gains. The report suggests reducing the proportion of earmarked grants. Other fiscal recommendations include revisiting land tax exemptions and criteria considered in transfers from the national government to reduce distortions.
- Providing quality public services – including public education – proves a challenge in shrinking areas. The report recommends that Estonia harness inter-municipal co-operation – currently only used on a limited scale – to improve the quality of services.
- Municipalities sometimes lack the tools they need to plan and implement service provision. The report highlights open information systems and administrative support as areas for attention.
- An increase in built areas is largely disconnected from local population trends – instead driven by, for example, second home ownership – which leads to inefficient land use. The report recommends that Estonia promote densification of central areas (town centres).
- Demolition and renovation projects are key targets for better planning, and should align with the countywide spatial plans.

Source: OECD (2022[16]), *Shrinking Smartly in Estonia: Preparing Regions for Demographic Change*, https://doi.org/10.1787/77cfe25e-en.

Two factors linked to migration contribute to population change in Estonia's regions. First, Estonian residents are leaving to live in the capital region. In 2023, the greatest net internal migration, i.e. migration among Estonian regions (Figure 1.3), could be found in North Estonia. In some regions, the outflow of population to the capital region is particularly pronounced: for example, 80% of internal migrants from Northeast Estonia migrated to North Estonia in 2021 (Statistics Estonia, 2022[20]). Data from 2017-23 (Annex B) show the same pattern holds over time,[5] with North Estonia leading in internal migration, although its lead has narrowed during this period. Second, although net external migration (international immigration) was generally positive in all regions between 2017 and 2023,[6] it is primarily concentrated in North Estonia. The region received the largest share of immigrants during this period, and nearly half of all international migrants who moved to Estonia in the last decade settled in Tallinn (OECD, 2022[16]; Statistics Estonia, 2022[20]). In short, even if external migration is generally net positive across all regions, it remains too limited outside of the capital region to compensate for natural population decline.

Figure 1.3. Net migration – both internal and external – is highest in the capital region

Net internal and external migration as a share of population by TL3 region, 2023

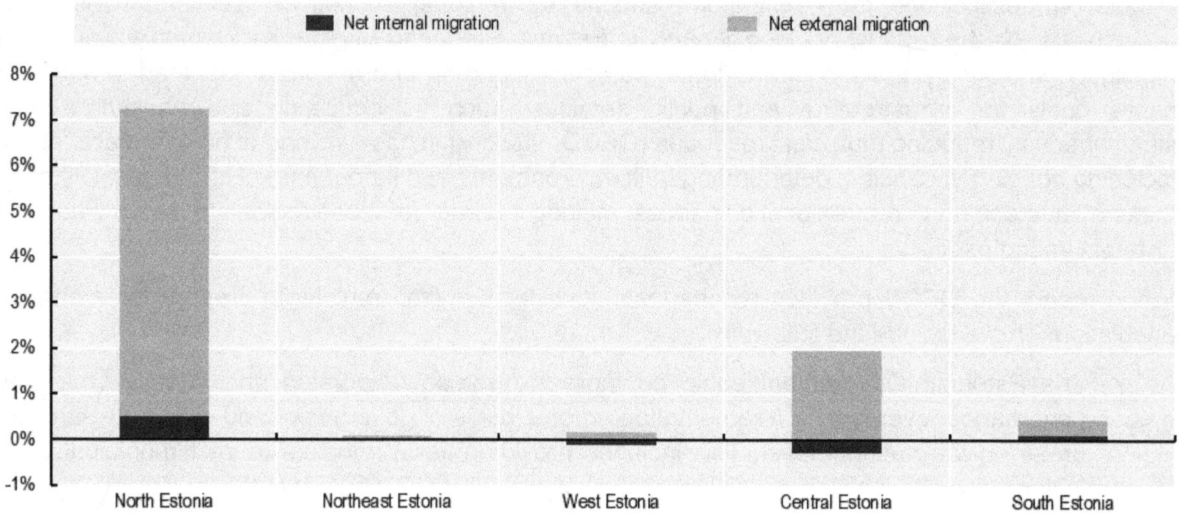

Source: Statistics Estonia (2023[21]), *RVR02: Migration by Administrative Unit/Type of Settlement Region, Sex, and Type of Migration*, https://andmed.stat.ee/en/stat/rahvastik__rahvastikusundmused__ranne/RVR02.

These settlement and demographic characteristics will affect the performance of Estonia's regions – not only in economic terms, but more broadly in socio-economic terms and overall well-being. The businesses regions can attract and retain, their available labour force, the distances travelled to and from jobs or education centres, and the services and amenities provided are all influenced by place (where regions and populations are located) and people (who lives in the regions). To advance the performance of a country or region, considering the unique characteristics of a place and its people (i.e. a place-based approach) is fundamental in order to more accurately respond to development needs. The following sections examine how regional differences in areas like gross domestic product (GDP), labour productivity, and specific dimensions of well-being may inform a place-based approach to territorial development.

The differentiated economic performance of Estonia's regions

There is a divide in economic performance among Estonian regions. The capital city of Tallinn – and the broader North Estonia region – has long acted as the country's primary economic driver, contributing over 60% of national GDP and consistently outperforming other regions in GDP per capita and productivity. While Tartu in South Estonia represents a secondary economic hub, most other regions offer a much smaller contribution to Estonia's economy. Nevertheless, all of the regions are distinct in their economic bases and examining these individually helps to explain the broader economic patterns considered in this section.

Estonian regions have distinct economic bases

Estonian regions differ in terms of what sectors are driving their economies. North Estonia stands out for its strong service economy, while Northeast Estonia is heavily reliant on industry, particularly the energy sector. Central and South Estonia show a more mixed economic structure, with notable roles for agriculture and manufacturing. West Estonia combines industrial activity with a substantial tourism-driven service sector. Table 1.2 describes the distinct profile of each region's economic bases, drawing on the value-added from services, industry and agriculture (Annex B). These differences provide context to interpret the regional economic performance data that follow. It is also important to bear in mind that North Estonia alone accounts for nearly two-thirds of Estonia's total value-added; South Estonia accounts for just under 19%, and Central, Northeast and West Estonia each contribute less than 10% (Annex B). These differences help contextualise sector shares: a high percentage in a smaller region may reflect specialisation in that sector, while in North Estonia, even a modest sector share corresponds to a large absolute value.

Table 1.2. Estonia's regions have different drivers of economic growth

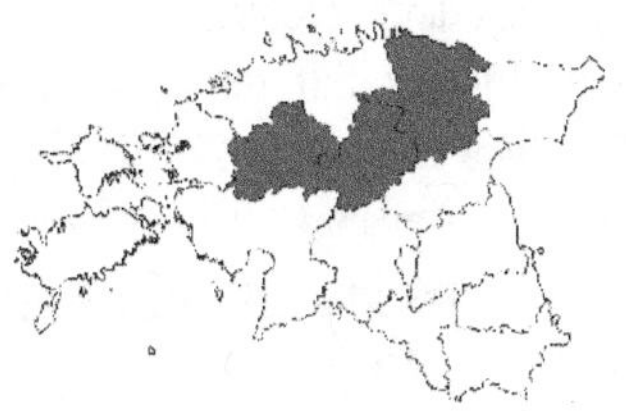	Central Estonia has a mixed economy with a notable share of agriculture. Its value-added from agriculture (9%) is the highest among all regions. While it is not the largest producer of Estonia's main agricultural products, cereals and milk – that distinction goes to South Estonia – it comes a close second (Statistics Estonia, 2019[22]; 2017[23]). The labour market in Central Estonia, however, is more dependent on the sector than that in other regions, with nearly 8% of employment in the agriculture, forestry and fishing sector alone in 2022 (compared to a national average of 3%) (OECD, 2022[24]). Activity in the industry (37%) and services (54%) sectors is also significant (Statistics Estonia, 2023[25]).
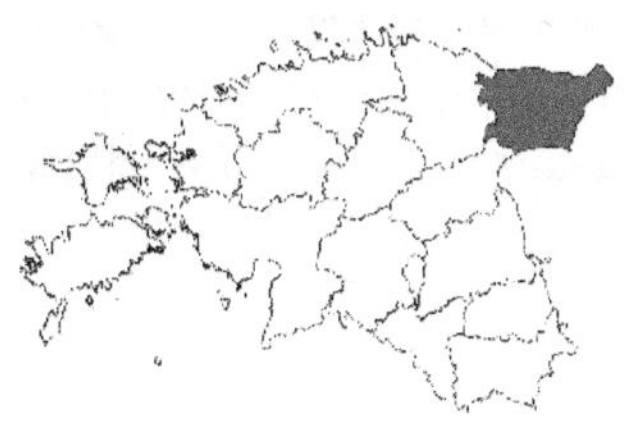	Northeast Estonia is the most industry-intensive region in the country, driven by its energy sector. Just over half (51%) of its value-added comes from industry and construction, driven primarily by its energy sector (Statistics Estonia, 2020[26]). The oil shale sector is the heart of the region's economy and 40% of the regions' largest employers are oil shale companies (EC, 2023[27]; Praxis, 2020[28]). Services account for 48%, the lowest share nationally (Statistics Estonia, 2023[25]). As discussed in greater depth in the section on labour markets, the region's dependence on one industrial sector makes it vulnerable to changes affecting the sector, whether market- or policy-driven (it is already experiencing changes due to the green transition).
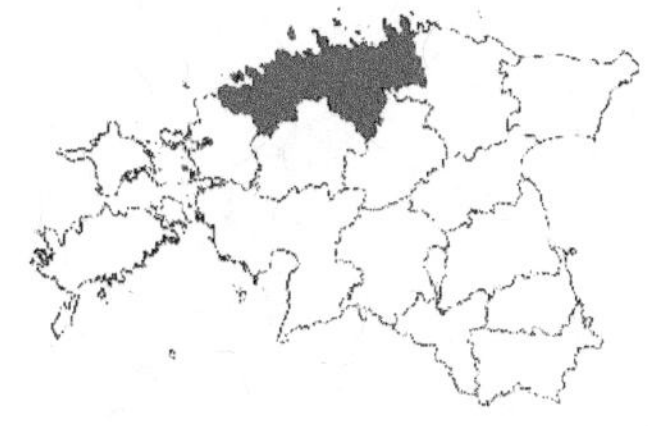	North Estonia – with the capital city Tallinn – has an economy that is dominated by the service sector. It generates about 81% of its value-added from services, driven by trade, information and communications, real estate and financial and insurance activities in the region (ERR, 2024[29]). Industry contributes 19% of the region's value-added – a smaller share than in other regions – led by manufacturing, energy and electronics. Agriculture is not an important contributor in this region (Statistics Estonia, 2023[25]; Invest in Estonia, n.d.[30]).
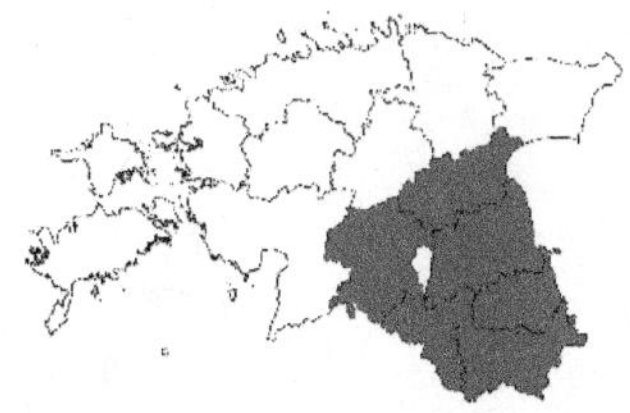	South Estonia is a service-oriented region, with its university town of Tartu. The service industry generates 68% of the region's value-added, anchored by Tartu's education, trade, health and real estate activities (ERR, 2023[31]). Industry accounts for 27% of its value-added, with large timber and food industries (Statistics Estonia, 2023[25]; Invest in Estonia, n.d.[32]). South Estonia is the country's top producer of wood and wood products (excluding furniture) and falls just behind North Estonia in furniture production (Statistics Estonia, 2023[33]) While South Estonia has a modest share of value-added from agriculture (5%), it is the country's top producer of

cereals, milk and many other agricultural products (Statistics Estonia, 2023[25]; 2019[22]; 2017[23]). It contains two of the most agriculturally intensive counties in Estonia, Jõgeva and Põlva (ERR, 2023[31]).

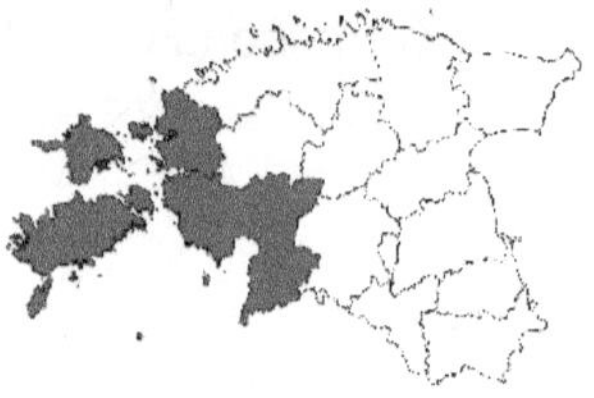

West Estonia is another region with a more mixed economy, with a substantial tourism industry. Services account for 63% of its value-added. Tourism is an especially important contributor to West Estonia's service sector. The region comes second only to North Estonia in the number of accommodated tourists: while North Estonia accommodated about half of tourists in 2023, West Estonia accommodated 21%. It surpasses South (17%), Northeast (6%) and Central (5%) Estonia (Statistics Estonia, 2023[34]). In addition to its substantial service sector, 31% of the region's value-added comes from industry (including forestry and wood processing). Agriculture is not a strong overall contributor but remains more prominent at 6% than in Northeast Estonia (1%) (Statistics Estonia, 2023[25]).

As Estonia considers a more placed-based approach to its development, it would be important to support growth based on the industrial capacities, assets and priorities of each region. While Estonia showed strong convergence with other OECD member countries before a recent economic downturn, there is scope for greater productivity convergence (Box 1.2). The sector compositions of the five regions suggest that different levers will need to be pushed to help further increase productivity. For instance, in Estonian regions with a strong manufacturing base, there may be particular opportunities to move up global value chains, where digitalisation can help firms (especially those with more routine tasks) capture more value and generate broader productivity spillovers (OECD, 2024[35]; Mosiashvili and Pareliussen, 2020[36]). A concerted effort to maximise the value of existing sectors can include working with regions to identify where investment could have the greatest impact in the short, medium and long terms – be it for efficiency, infrastructure, innovation or human capital.

Box 1.2. How has the Estonian economy performed overall?

An economic downturn followed years of convergence, but recovery is expected soon

After a relatively severe economic downturn beginning in 2022, driven by trade disruptions, weaker export demand, high inflation and tight monetary conditions, the Estonian economy is expected to begin recovering as external demand improves. Since 2000, living standards in Estonia have doubled and the country made steady progress in income convergence prior to the pandemic. Nevertheless, per capita GDP and productivity still remain below OECD averages. The 2024 OECD Economic Survey of Estonia cites "[delivering] an economic recovery and return to stronger growth and economic convergence, while ensuring more inclusive outcomes" as an objective for Estonia (OECD, 2024[35])..

Figure 1.4. Estonia's economy is experiencing a relatively severe downturn

Real GDP, Estonia and OECD, 2015-24

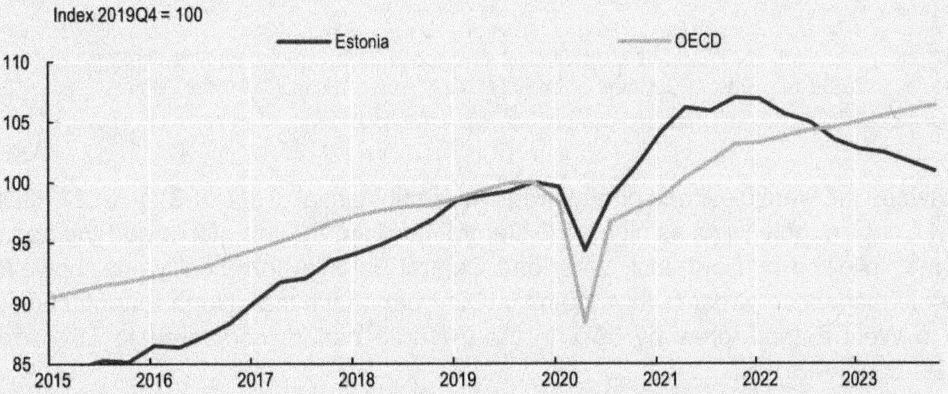

Source: OECD (n.d.[37]), *OECD Economic Outlook Database*, https://www.oecd.org/en/topics/economic-outlook.html.

There is scope for greater productivity convergence

Estonia has made strong progress towards convergence in productivity with OECD peers over the past decades, but growth slowed before the pandemic and has become more volatile since. The country still lags in labour productivity, with a 30% gap to the upper half of OECD countries due to weak multifactor productivity. With an already-high employment rate, reviving productivity growth will be important to support future gains in living standards. As discussed further in the next section, additional productivity gains can be realised through integrating into global value chains and moving up value chains (including through improvements in digitalisation).

Sources: OECD (n.d.[37]), *OECD Economic Outlook Database*, https://www.oecd.org/en/topics/economic-outlook.html; OECD (2024[35]), *OECD Economic Surveys: Estonia 2024*, https://doi.org/10.1787/33e6beee-en.

Economic activity concentrates in North Estonia

Economic data for Estonia's regions reveal large differences among regions in terms of GDP, GDP per capita and productivity. North Estonia stands out as the clear economic hub, accounting for 62% of Estonia's GDP (Table 1.3). That most of the value of goods and services in Estonia comes from North Estonia may reflect a concentration of high-value firms (e.g., finance, information and communication technology), skilled workers, infrastructure and institutions in Tallinn and its surroundings. South Estonia's economy, while substantially smaller than that of North Estonia, comes second, accounting for 19% of GDP. The remaining 3 regions generate 6-7% of GDP each (Statistics Estonia, 2023[38]). Combined, these figures show just how dominant the capital region is in the national economy.

Table 1.3. Economic indicators of Estonia's regions

TL3 regions and whole country, 2023

	GDP at current prices (EUR billion)	Share of GDP in Estonia (%)	GDP, change 2018-23 (%)	GDP per capita (EUR)	GDP per capita, change 2018-23 (%)
Central Estonia	2.2	6	40	18 000	41
Northeast Estonia	2.6	7	37	19 800	42
North Estonia	23.6	62	44	36 800	33
South Estonia	7.1	19	50	22 000	48
West Estonia	2.7	7	49	18 100	50
Estonia (whole country)	38.2	100	44	28 000	40

Source: Eurostat (2023[39]), *Gross Domestic Product (GDP) at Current Market Prices by NUTS 3 Region*, https://ec.europa.eu/eurostat/databrowser/view/nama_10r_3gdp$defaultview/default/table.

The gap between the wealthiest and poorest regions is substantial (Table 1.3): in 2023, GDP per capita in North Estonia was roughly twice as high as in Central Estonia. South Estonia had the second largest per capita income, followed by Northeast, West and Central Estonia. In recent years, however, non-capital regions have experienced larger relative gains in GDP per capita than North Estonia. For example, GDP per capita in West Estonia grew by 50% in the 2018-23 period, compared to 33% in North Estonia (Eurostat, 2023[39]).

In 2020, Estonia was among the OECD countries[7] with the greatest disparities in labour productivity between metropolitan regions and regions far from cities (OECD, 2022[40]). In 2022, productivity in Estonia's top region (North Estonia, with a gross value added [GVA] per worker[8] of USD 84 279) was nearly 53%[9] higher than that of the least-productive region (West Estonia, with a GVA per worker of USD 55 224)[10] (Figure 1.5) (OECD, 2022[41]). Regions that are far from cities – Central and West Estonia (see Figure 1.1) – have the lowest overall labour productivity.

Sector-specific labour productivity data tends to reflect the same pattern (Annex B). The lead position of North Estonia in labour productivity is consistent across most sectors, with the effects of agglomeration (discussed further below) as one potential contributor.[11] Northeast Estonia currently leads in industry (excluding construction) and manufacturing, likely reflecting, in part, the concentration of oil shale activity in the region. It also led in agriculture in 2022, though this appears to reflect the small size and volatility of the sector rather than a consistent labour productivity advantage in the region over time. However, it lags behind other regions in the labour productivity of construction. South Estonia shows mid-range performance across most sectors and leads in the labour productivity of real estate activities. Central Estonia shows relatively strong labour productivity in construction, manufacturing and agriculture, but lower productivity across the other sectors. West Estonia has the lowest labour productivity across several sectors,[12] but is middle-of-the-pack when it comes to: construction; professional, scientific and technical activities; and arts, entertainment and recreation, other service activities, activities of household and extra-territorial organisations and bodies. These patterns highlight that regional disparities in productivity are not only due to differences in sector composition but also to differences in productivity among firms within sectors.

North Estonia's labour productivity has fluctuated in recent years, with a percent change of 0% between 2018 and 2022. In the same period, West Estonia's labour productivity grew more than in any other region (Figure 1.5). This is consistent with a broader trend among OECD member countries: while capital regions often lead in productivity levels, the fastest productivity growth in many countries has occurred in non-capital regions (OECD, 2022[40]). In Estonia, however, non-capital regions still have a long way to go before they can match North Estonia's labour productivity.

Figure 1.5. Regional disparities in labour productivity persist, despite improvements in non-capital regions

Labour productivity, national average and TL3 regions, GVA per person employed, 2018-22

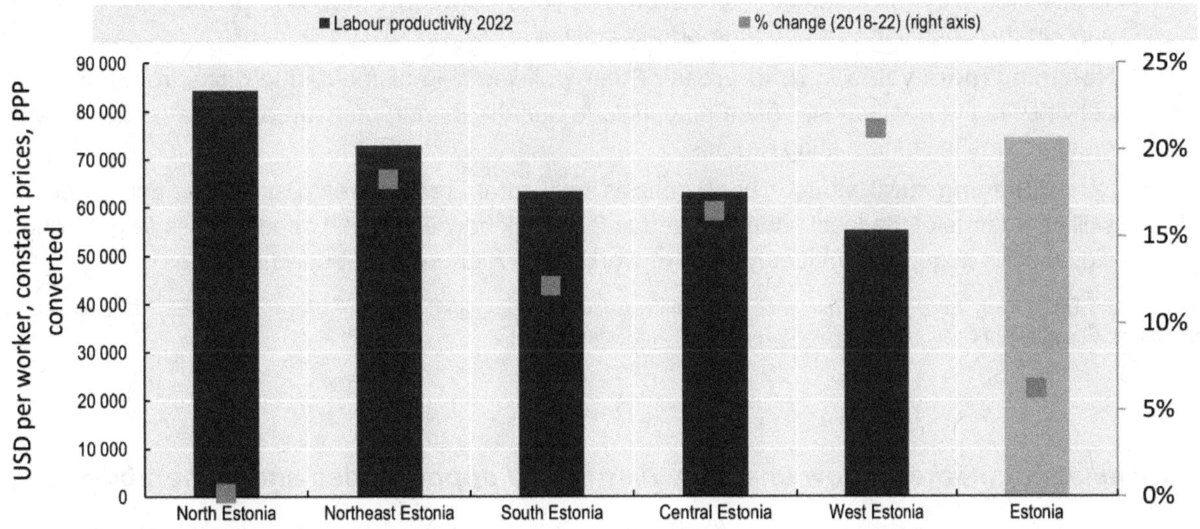

Note: PPP: purchasing power parity.
Source: OECD (2022[41]), *Regions, Cities and Local Statistics*, https://www.oecd.org/en/topics/regions-cities-and-local-statistics.html.

Large differences in labour productivity among regions – and among sectors in regions – point to a potential role for place-specific interventions to boost performance. Addressing differences in labour productivity requires that policy makers take into account the different characteristics of different regions. For example, metropolitan regions generally have a built-in advantage for productivity: agglomeration effects mean that factors like shared infrastructure, higher quality public services and knowledge spillovers offer benefits that drive productivity growth. Other regions, especially rural ones, do not benefit from these advantages. Given the large structural differences across regions, it is "unrealistic to fully eradicate all inequality in productivity" (OECD, 2023[42]). However, these gaps can be narrowed through approaches that account for the distinct characteristics and economic profiles of each region. This rationale underpins the policies to increase rural productivity in Box 1.3.

Policy makers stand to benefit from considering labour productivity across all regions. Improving the productivity of regions has implications for national productivity: the productivity of peripheral and even lagging regions can contribute to aggregate productivity (Garcilazo and Oliveira Martins, 2013[43]). Doing so can also deliver benefits beyond productivity growth alone. Regions with high productivity tend to have greater resources, a better ability to provide better material conditions for workers (through quality employment and higher wages), as well as more effective public services, all of which contribute to the well-being of the region's population (Tsvetkova et al., 2020[44]; OECD, 2020[45]).

Box 1.3. Policies for rural productivity

The OECD emphasises that rural policies should be designed through a place-based approach: tailored to the unique characteristics of each area, taking into account, for example, its specific assets, key industries, labour mobility constraints and connections to nearby cities. This is evident in policies to increase rural productivity, which can be grouped into four main areas:

- **Building value in tradeable activities**: These policies encourage rural regions to move up the value chain in tradeable sectors (like manufacturing, agriculture and tradeable services). These may include enabling smart specialisation and diversification in rural economies, fostering innovation ecosystems in rural areas and supporting productivity increases in rural companies.
- **Helping small and medium-sized enterprises (SMEs) access global value chains**: Policies in this area may, for example, favour greater links between SMEs and global companies or support the transition to high-value-added activities.
- **Retaining more value in rural areas**: These policies help distribute the gains from tradeable activities to the population. These may include benefit-sharing measures, like revenue transfer mechanisms in some mining regions.
- **Strengthening rural skills**: These policies help rural areas develop skills that can meet the skills demands of the local economy and help unlock new economic opportunities (e.g. through digital skills acquisition that can prepare workers for higher-value-added activities).

Sources: OECD (2018[46]), "Rural 3.0: A Framework for Rural Development", https://doi.org/10.1787/618f702b-en; OECD (2020[47]), *Rural Well-being: Geography of Opportunities*, https://doi.org/10.1787/d25cef80-en.

Regional labour markets show unevenly distributed opportunities and vulnerabilities

Labour market data for Estonia's regions paint a picture of uneven labour market outcomes. The data show differences in employment and participation, as well as pointing to some areas where individuals may not match with vacancies efficiently. These differences are most pronounced between North Estonia and other regions. Combined, these figures may indicate that labour market potential in lagging regions is underutilised. At the same time, a lack of employment diversification in some regions may increase vulnerability to shocks affecting the sectors that are these regions' biggest employers (OECD, 2021[48]). Demographic change, which is projected to hit hardest in regions already facing weaker labour market outcomes, may dampen growth in the years to come (Bodnár and Nerlich, 2022[49]). These labour market disparities, especially when compounded by demographic change, may influence the long-term growth prospects of Estonia's regions in different ways.

Northeast Estonia faces the greatest labour market challenges. The employment rate has been lower outside of North Estonia in recent years, with Northeast Estonia consistently having the lowest employment rate (Figure 1.6) (OECD, 2023[50]; Statistics Estonia, 2024[51]). Northeast Estonia also has the highest share of unemployed individuals in the labour force: 14.3%. While the Northeast is an outlier, the unemployment rate of other regions does not differ significantly as of most recent data (ranging from nearly 7% in South Estonia to 8% in West Estonia in 2024) (Eesti Pank, 2024[52]; Statistics Estonia, 2024[51]). Northeast Estonia's labour market challenges can be explained in part by the decline of region's oil shale industry, which has historically been a major employer in the region (Ferraro and Kommer, 2023[53]).

Figure 1.6. Northeast Estonia has a considerably lower employment rate than the other regions

Employment rate for 15-74 year-olds, national average and TL3 regions, 2018-24

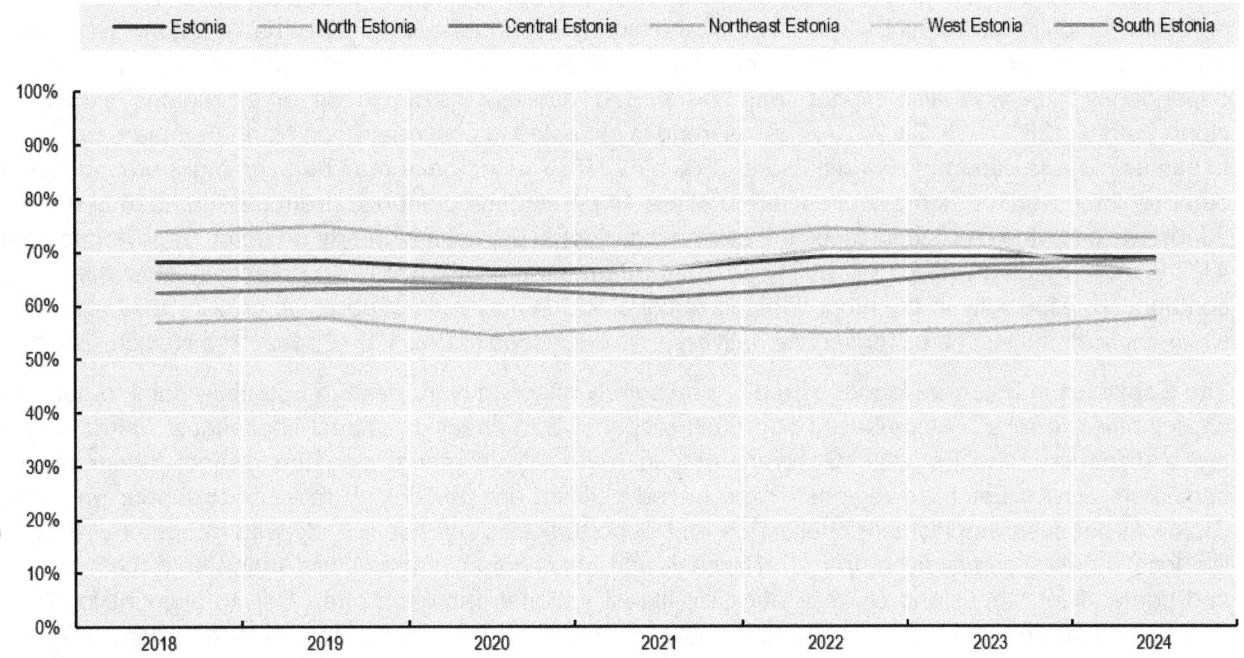

Note: This time series begins in 2018, the first year for which Statistics Estonia has compiled regional employment data.
Source: Statistics Estonia (2024[51]), *TT4645: Labour Status of Population Aged 15-74 by Region, County and Age Group*, https://andmed.stat.ee/en/stat/sotsiaalelu__tooturg__tooturu-uldandmed__aastastatistika/TT4645.

Northeast Estonia shows signs of a labour market mismatch, where unemployed individuals are matching with job vacancies less efficiently than in other regions. The county of Ida-Viru (which corresponds to the region of Northeast Estonia) has a significantly higher unemployment rate than the national average, as well as the lowest matching efficiency, a proxy for mismatch in the labour market between job seekers and vacancies. In an index of matching efficiency,[13] the county of Ida-Viru receives 0.8 while Harju county (which corresponds to the region of North Estonia) receives 1.0 (Ferraro and Kommer, 2023[53]). The regional labour market mismatch that these data suggest is likely driven in part by a decline in oil shale and mining industries, which have historically dominated the local economy and are now contracting due to national and European Union (EU) climate goals (Fina, Heider and Masso, 2021[54]). Hiiu, Valga and Võru counties in West and South Estonia also show signs that the unemployed struggle to find suitable vacancies, which may relate more to their seasonal employment (in West Estonia) and distance from Tallinn (in South Estonia) (Ferraro and Kommer, 2023[53]). Supporting this, Estonian Government data confirm that job availability commensurate to education, skills and needs is lowest in the county of Ida-Viru (Northeast Estonia) and sparsely populated regions (Estonian Ministry of Finance, 2021, p. 8[18]).

A low degree of diversification in the mix of sectors forming the economic base in some regions increases their vulnerability to decline or disruption. In several regions, employment tends to be concentrated in just a few sectors. In Central Estonia, for example, 54% of the workforce was employed in industry and manufacturing in 2022. Northeast and West Estonia follow right behind, with around 50% of their workforces employed in industry and manufacturing (OECD, 2022[55]). This may leave the labour market of these regions vulnerable to shocks affecting these sectors (as the labour market of Northeast Estonia has already proved vulnerable to the transition away from oil shale (OECD, 2021[48]).

Demographic trends may exacerbate regional labour market challenges. A declining working-age population and a growing ageing population are projected to slow Estonia's potential growth in the coming years (OECD, 2024[35]). This will be felt differently in different regions. The old-age dependency ratio, which measures the proportion of elderly people relative to the working-age population (those aged 15-64), is particularly high in Northeast Estonia: in 2021, the elderly dependency rate in Northeast Estonia was nearly 43%, meaning there were 43 elderly individuals for every 100 working-age individuals. The old-age dependency rate was also higher than the OECD average (30%) in all other regions except for North Estonia (28%) (OECD, 2023[50]). This trend is expected to continue. Even North Estonia is projected to see its old-age dependency ratio rise to 33% by 2040. The increase may be even more pronounced in other regions: South Estonia is expected to see a 14 percentage point rise (from 33% in 2020 to 47% by 2040), while Northeast Estonia faces the steepest projected increase of nearly 34 percentage points (from 41% to 75% by 2040) (Eurostat, 2021[56]). These demographic changes can potentially slow the labour contribution, especially in the most affected regions, which may restrict potential growth (they also have wider implications – such as for service delivery – as discussed in Box 1.1) (Bodnár and Nerlich, 2022[49]).

The disparities in Estonia's labour market – particularly affecting Northeastern Estonia – point to potential opportunities to take a place-based approach responsive to specific regional challenges. In addressing these disparities, the Estonian Government can benefit from recognising the distinct labour market conditions across Estonia's regions. Place-based policies are particularly relevant to labour and skills (Box 1.4) because employment challenges and opportunities vary significantly with geography. Factors like local industry composition, transport access and educational infrastructure shape both the supply of and demand for labour and skills. A one-size-fits-all national approach often fails to account for these variations (Green, 2023[57]). Place-based policies, on the other hand, can help to address spatial mismatches between firms and regions (OECD, 2025[3]). In Estonia, this could, for example, take the shape of policies to increase the flow of investment and jobs to regions other than the capital region (Ferraro and Kommer, 2023[53]), based on the regions' industrial and skills compositions.

Box 1.4. Place-based labour and skills policies: Neighbourhood employment support policies

Neighbourhood-level employment policies aim to bring employment services directly into communities that need them, making them easier to access and more relevant to local needs. These policies are particularly relevant for addressing entrenched labour market disadvantages in small areas, where challenges are both complex and long-lasting. These areas often face fragmented service provision that is difficult to navigate not just for individuals, but also for employers and policy makers. Place-based interventions at this scale can provide holistic support that is responsive to community needs. To be effective, however, these policies must be connected to broader systems, with feedback loops to national policy.

Neighbourhood employment hubs are one example of a place-based intervention for labour and skills. These hubs offer multiple services in the same location that are accessible and tailored to local needs. They integrate employment assistance, skills training and often additional support such as childcare or transport advice. Another approach involves using discretionary local funding to design initiatives that directly target specific barriers to employment within communities, for example improving job accessibility in disconnected neighbourhoods, developing "pathways to employment" with local employers or offering targeted training for the long-term unemployed.

Source: Green, A. (2023[57]), "When should place-based policies be used and at what scale?", https://www.oecd.org/cfe/regionaldevelopment/place-based-policies-for-thefuture.htm.

Conclusion: A country of distinct regional economies but one economic engine

The data in this section show that North Estonia, the country's capital region, remains the country's economic engine and has pulled far ahead on most economic indicators (including GDP and productivity). It also shows that Estonia's other regions have distinct economic structures and varying growth trajectories. Despite promising signs of economic growth in recent years (for example, in West Estonia), non-capital regions have remained behind. The data also show how major transformations have affected or are expected to affect Estonia's regions differently (OECD, 2025[3]), such as in economic and labour market challenges facing Northeast Estonia with the green transition and non-capital regions with demographic change. These differences can help to reveal potential opportunities for place-based policy to respond to the specific characteristics, assets and challenges of Estonian regions. As the next section will show, regional gaps in a number of well-being dimensions highlight the potential for a more place-based approach to help address non-economic outcomes across Estonia, as well.

Designing and implementing policy or programmes to help less-performing regions boost their performance, while also fostering growth among strong performers, are not mutually exclusive endeavours. To do so successfully, however, can depend on actively pursuing a place-based approach where regional assets, needs and constraints are considered in tandem with national development objectives. For Estonia, this may take the shape of place-based approaches to help address spatial mismatches and underutilised assets, tailored to the unique features of each place, including labour market structures, sector specialisations and institutional capacity (OECD, 2025[3]).

Enablers for regional well-being in Estonia's regions

How is life in Estonia's regions? To answer this question, this section delves into 3 aspects of the 11 dimensions of regional well-being studied by the OECD. Examining these well-being dimensions complements the economic and labour market indicators presented earlier by assessing whether prosperity is, in fact, translating into better lives (OECD, 2014[58]). While each region will interpret and prioritise well-being dimensions differently based on its development goals, identifying where disparities exist – and what may be driving them – can help both levels of government in Estonia consider how to integrate well-being considerations into their regional development efforts. In particular, it can help show areas where line ministries (such as those responsible for labour, transport, health, education, housing and related areas) can consider more regionally sensitive approaches to policy design and implementation.

This section zooms in on three aspects of well-being: health, education and transport connectivity. Each of these areas can either help or hinder regional development. The health of a region's population is a critical factor in regional development, directly affecting people's quality of life and productivity. Education also plays a crucial role, equipping individuals with skills necessary for employment and creating human capacity for innovation. Finally, transport connectivity is an enabler for regional development by improving access to health services, education and jobs (OECD, 2014[58]).

Among Estonia's regions, gaps in these three areas risk holding back regional development if left unaddressed. Disparities in healthcare access and outcomes, uneven educational access, attainment and skills, and poor transport connectivity – particularly in rural areas – may restrict the ability of residents of some regions to live fulfilled lives and contribute to the development of their region. Place-based policies that are responsive to local needs may have a role to play in addressing these disparities.

Uneven health outcomes and access to healthcare services across Estonia's regions

North Estonia consistently performs better than the other regions in most major health indicators, apart from infant mortality, while Northeast Estonia tends to fare the worst. Regional differences in access to healthcare services also shape health inequalities among Estonian regions. As rural populations are projected to age more rapidly in Estonia, these disparities are expected to place even greater strain on health systems in those regions. Importantly, the nature of these pressures may differ from one region to another, depending on factors such as healthcare infrastructure and baseline population health. This means that a single national health policy or intervention may not effectively address the diverse healthcare challenges across the country, especially as demographic pressures play out differently across regions. The following section considers regional health and healthcare patterns in greater detail, highlighting that addressing these challenges may require a place-based approach that takes into account the unique conditions of each area to ensure that policies and interventions are better aligned with local needs.

The capital region tends to fare better in terms of health outcomes than the other regions. In 2022, there was nearly a 5-year gap in life expectancy between North Estonia and Northeast Estonia (OECD, 2025[59]). The difference in disability-free life expectancy between the highest- and lowest-performing region was more striking: nearly 12 years between North Estonia (62.3 years) and Northeast Estonia (50.7 years) (Statistics Estonia, 2022[60]). In other words, people in Northeast Estonia may live nearly as long as those in North Estonia, but they spend more of their lives with a limiting long-term illness. Obesity rates in 2016 were also notably higher in Central and South Estonia (nearly 22%) compared to North Estonia (around 16%). Infant mortality in 2017 was lowest in West Estonia (1.5 deaths per 1 000 live births) and highest in Northeast Estonia (4 deaths per 1 000 live births) (OECD, 2025[59]). The best and worst performing regions differ depending on the indicator, but the data suggest that health outcomes tend to be better in the capital region.

Healthcare access – measured in terms of healthcare staff and hospital beds – also varies across Estonia's regions. Access to healthcare is shaped in part by the availability of healthcare professionals. In 2021, Central Estonia had just over 2 active physicians per 1 000 inhabitants, while South Estonia had around 5. Similarly, there were fewer than 4 practicing nurses per 1 000 inhabitants in Central Estonia, compared to over 8 in South Estonia. Hospital bed availability follows the same pattern, with around 3 beds per 1 000 inhabitants in Central Estonia, and 6 in South Estonia (OECD, 2025[59]). Experts expect that ageing populations in Estonia's rural regions – as well as an ageing workforce of doctors (OECD/European Observatory on Health Systems and Policies, 2023[61]) – will add greater pressure on health systems in these regions in the future (OECD, 2024[35]).

Disparities in health outcomes and healthcare access across Estonia have prompted experts to call for approaches that are tailored to regional needs. These approaches recognise that social, economic and environmental conditions in the places people live and work shape health outcomes and that policies tailored to different regions can help to reduce inequalities. A major focus in Estonia is the uneven distribution of healthcare workers, especially in regions outside of North and South Estonia. The OECD Economic Survey of Estonia (2024[35]) recommends expanding financial incentives in underserved areas to support the creation of primary health centres and attract staff, including doctors and nurses. Estonia has begun to move in this direction: it has already introduced regional salary differentiation and co-operation agreements between health colleges and regional hospitals – such as those between Tartu Health Care College and Narva Hospital – aim to expand nursing training outside of urban centres (OECD, 2024[35]).

Educational outcomes are highest in the capital region

There are significant regional disparities in educational attainment, access to higher education and adult skills across Estonia. North Estonia outperforms other regions in terms of educational attainment and literacy, while Central and Northeast Estonia tend to fall behind. These disparities are shaped in part by geography: higher education institutions and vocational schools are heavily concentrated in the urban centres of Tallinn and Tartu, limiting post-secondary options elsewhere and encouraging youth outmigration from less-served regions. In addition, some regions suffer from teacher shortages – especially in rural areas – which can affect the quality of education. Education access and quality affect the ability of regions to build human capital. The following section explores these patterns in more detail, highlighting where place-based policy can play a role in ensuring that education serves as a driver of regional development in all regions.

While Estonia tends to perform well on skills assessments overall (OECD, 2023[62]), significant regional gaps in literacy could limit the ability of individuals in some regions to find good jobs. Northeast Estonia has the lowest reading proficiency and North Estonia has the highest. Proficiency is measured on a scale where 500 represents the highest possible score, and scores are reported as ranges based on a 95% confidence interval. North Estonia scores 289-292, placing it in Proficiency Level III. In contrast, Northeast Estonia scores 238-244, which falls in the lower part of Level II, a full skill level below. The second highest performing region is South Estonia (274-278), on the threshold between Levels II and III, followed by West Estonia (266-271) and Central Estonia (257-262). These differences are not only large but also statistically significant across all regions, showing clear regional differences in adult literacy skills (Estonian Ministry of Education and Research, 2023[63]). Weaknesses in skills have a bearing on an individual's ability to access quality jobs, participate fully in the labour market and contribute to the economic development of their regions. In addition, these gaps risk becoming self-reinforcing, as Estonia shows a strong link between adults' skills and their parents' education levels, meaning that the concentration of low-skilled individuals in certain regions may perpetuate disadvantage across generations (ERR, 2024[64]).

North Estonia stands out with the highest share of residents holding a tertiary degree (51%) and the lowest share with only basic education (8%), with very little change in these figures from 2017 to 2021 (Figure 1.7). Patterns of tertiary education attainment follow the concentration of universities and enrolment in higher education in North and South Estonia. Tallinn in North Estonia and Tartu in South Estonia dominate the higher education landscape. The main campuses of Estonia's universities are all in these 2 regions: North Estonia hosts 11[14] and Tartu hosts 6[15] (Study In Estonia, 2024[65]). For this reason, enrolment in higher education is much higher in North and South Estonia than in the other regions. In the metropolitan region of North Estonia, there are nearly 60 higher education students per 1 000 inhabitants, compared to just under 39 in Central and West Estonia, regions located far from an FUA (Figure 1.1) (OECD, 2024[66]). Regions outside of North and South Estonia still have universities, but they tend to be branches of institutions based in Tallinn or Tartu.[16] The concentration of universities and university enrolment in North and South Estonia gives these regions an edge in regional educational attainment (Russell, Yu and Andrews, 2021[67]).

Figure 1.7. Educational attainment by region

Educational attainment by TL3 region, percent of the population from 25 to 65 years, 2021

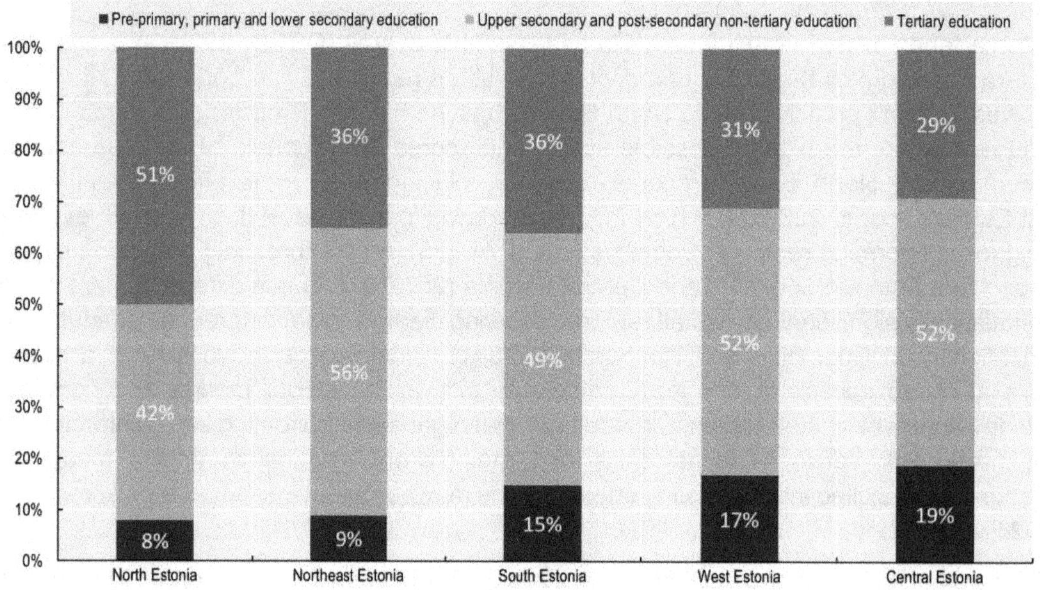

Source: OECD (2025[68]), *Educational Attainment - Regions*, http://data-explorer.oecd.org/s/1l0.

Similarly, the number of vocational schools in a region and enrolment in vocational programmes goes hand in hand, with North and South Estonia leading in school availability and student numbers. North Estonia has the highest enrolment in vocational education, accounting for more than a third of all vocational students (10 106 students) and hosting the largest number of vocational schools (13). South Estonia also has substantial enrolment in vocational programmes (8 472 students) and a relatively large number of schools (11 schools). In contrast, Central and Western Estonia show more modest enrolment, with around 3 300 students each (3 323 and 3 228 respectively) and a smaller number of schools (4 and 5). Northeastern Estonia stands out for its low figures on both fronts, with just 2 475 students and only 1 vocational school (Statistics Estonia, 2024[69]).

These figures show how access to education may inadvertently encourage outmigration of youth from other regions to North and South Estonia. Post-secondary educational opportunities – both vocational and higher education – are concentrated in North and South Estonia. As a result, youth in other areas often must leave home to continue their studies, regardless of the path they choose. This effect is felt most keenly in rural areas: a 2001 paper found that in particularly poorly-served counties – Hiiu, Järva, Rapla and Valga – more than four out of five students reported a lack of suitable vocational training opportunities. As the authors of the report observed, Estonian education is "a channel that primarily leads young people to leave their rural homes" (Dsiss and Taru, 2001[70]).

Rural areas face the greatest difficulties in attracting and retaining qualified teachers (Estonian Ministry of Education and Research, 2023[71]). In 2018, nearly half (44%) of rural teachers worked part-time compared to just 28% in urban schools, which may be due to small school sizes and limited capacity to offer full-time positions. Rural areas also struggled with the retention of teachers: teachers in rural schools were more likely to express an intention to leave the profession, with 30% of rural teachers reporting plans to exit, compared to 22% in Tallinn. Rural teachers also reported feeling their profession was less valued by society: only 23% of rural teachers believed their role was respected, compared to 29% of their peers in larger cities (Estonian Ministry of Education and Research, 2020[72]). These factors, combined with an ageing teaching workforce in many rural municipalities, risk reinforcing educational inequalities between regions and undermining efforts to ensure equitable access to quality education across the country. A shortage of qualified teachers can worsen the quality of education in areas that are most affected (Estonian National Audit Office, 2024[73]), which in turn constrains the development of human capital in these regions.

The provision of education in Estonia appears to be strongly influenced by territorial characteristics and the current concentration of opportunity in a few urban centres risks reinforcing regional inequalities. The data suggest that there are regions – particularly Central, Northeast and West Estonia – where targeted national support can help overcome regional disparities in educational attainment, skills and access. One target for place-based action by the Estonian Government may be a shortage of teachers and support specialists in some regions, especially rural areas, that poses a challenge for equity in education across Estonia (Fina, Heider and Masso, 2021[54]). Experts recommend using evidence-based workforce planning tools to better forecast regional teacher needs and to link this to training provision and recruitment strategies. Estonia has made moves in this direction; for example, the Ministry of Education and Research has increased scholarship opportunities and teacher training places in recent years, and piloted salary increases (e.g. a 30% salary raise in Ida-Viru county) to attract qualified teachers to underserved regions (Leijen et al., 2024[74]). This type of targeted national government action could improve teacher supply in regions where shortages are greatest.

Rural areas have the lowest transport connectivity

Regional disparities in transport connectivity among Estonian regions may limit the ability of rural residents to access jobs and essential services. While residents of cities benefit from frequent and accessible public transport, access is much more limited in rural areas. Expanding public transport coverage to towns and rural areas can play a strong role in supporting well-being, particularly for those without access to a private car, as service provision and opportunity are closely linked to transport access (OECD, 2024[75]). In a country like Estonia – where much of the territory is rural – ensuring good regional connectivity is central to economic participation, social inclusion and territorial cohesion. After all, well-being hinges not just on the presence of jobs and services, but also on people's ability to reach them. The following section considers these patterns in more detail and explores how a place-based approach to transport can support regional development by improving mobility and access across all parts of the country.

In Estonia, rural areas are affected the most by low public transport access. A 2018 study revealed that only 17% of the rural population lived within 500 meters of a public transport stop that offers at least 1 departure per hour during the working day, compared to 92-99% in urban areas like Narva, Tallinn and Tartu (EFGS, 2018[76]). The Estonian Government's 2021 Transport and Mobility Development Plan acknowledges that poor transport access is a key barrier for residents in peripheral areas, limiting their opportunities to participate fully in the economy and social life (Estonian Ministry of Economic Affairs and Communications, 2020[77]).

These disparities in connectivity suggest a potential role for place-based policy in improving transport access to support regional development. A place-based approach in this policy area can start with co-ordinated planning among levels, something the Estonian Government is already seeking to improve. It has recognised that a disconnect in planning among the national and local levels is a barrier to improving transport services in its Transport and Mobility Development Plan, and underscored the importance of co-ordinated strategy among local authorities and the national government (Estonian Ministry of Economic Affairs and Communications, 2020, p. 26[77]). In addition, experts have come forward with other ideas to better connect underserved areas. For example, in rural and low-density areas, where traditional fixed-route services struggle to remain viable, there is particular potential to expand the use of demand-responsive transport systems (Soe, Atiullah Saif and Agriesti, 2022[78]). By tailoring transport approaches to local conditions in this way, Estonia can help to ensure that mobility is not a barrier for the well-being of its rural residents.

Conclusion: Minding the gaps in regional well-being outcomes

Regional disparities – both between the capital region and other regions, and among non-capital regions – are one justification for taking a place-based approach in Estonia. In many of the economic indicators highlighted in the previous section, the greatest differences tend to be between the capital region and other regions in Estonia. For these indicators – including indicators of regional GDP and labour productivity – if you remove the capital region, the other regions begin to look quite similar. For other indicators – like healthcare access and obesity – there is a greater degree of variability among the regions. Differences among regions are one justification for place-based policy, but not the only one. Regardless of whether regional disparities are large or small, regions differ in how they approach development, what they prioritise and what they have to offer. The next section shows that Estonian regions are not only defined by their needs but also by the assets they can build upon and the ambitions they have for the future. Place-based policy can help align national action with those assets and ambitions to help regions develop.

Capitalising on regional differences: Different visions, different tools in Central and South Estonia

Recognising the territorial differences that already exist in Estonia – from GDP per capita and labour productivity to well-being indicators – sets the foundation for understanding how the development aspirations of individual regions can differ, even when the overall objective is economic growth and resident well-being. Delivering on these diverse aspirations – be it through national or subnational strategies, plans or programmes – will require regionally adapted or appropriate policy tools grounded in a place-based policy approach. Place-based regional development policy aims to take advantage of a territory's development potential, by "[d]efining clear objectives based on a deep understanding of current and future needs, characteristics and assets of a place to unlock new pathways for development" (OECD, 2025, p. 58[3]). This means that the national government can apply its policy levers in a way is aligned with how regions experience specific policy challenges (e.g. the economic, labour market and well-being outcomes featured in the previous sections) and that promotes the advantages of each region. Doing so requires working closely with local stakeholders and residents, and even using bottom-up approaches in policy design, where local priorities flow more readily into national decision making through processes like co-design and delivery (OECD, 2025[3]).

This section is a short case study, exploring the regional development aspirations and assets identified by Central and South Estonia. It features these two regions as they both host a pilot regional council and have developed draft regional development agreements identifying how parties will work together to meet their regions' development ambitions (see Chapter 3). The OECD worked closely with the pilot regional councils throughout the course of the Strengthening Regional Specialisation and Competitiveness in Estonia project, including through foresight and vision-setting workshops with the two regions (Annex A). This process offered a view of how each region defines its own development ambitions and how these ambitions were translated into practical commitments in the draft agreements. It also offered a view of what assets the regions could capitalise upon to help enable regional development. This section gives insights into the ambitions and assets of the regions and how place-based policy can support them. While the section does explore three notable assets for development in the region - education, housing and quality of life - examining exactly how each region can increase its output or productivity by improving on or developing new firms and industries based on existing assets is beyond the scope of this report.

Central and South Estonia have their own ambitions for the development of their regions

During OECD workshops, the two regions sketched out a range of desired futures for their regions. The goal of these workshops was not to arrive at a single vision statement, but rather to explore what characteristics different desirable future scenarios would have. These ambitions (Table 1.4) can be broadly defined into three groups: people, environment and surroundings and business and economy. The regions' development ambitions in each of these three areas show that they are seeking opportunities to build on their regional strengths, as well as addressing some of the weaknesses identified in the previous sections.

Table 1.4. Development ambitions in Central and South Estonia

	Central Estonia	South Estonia
People	**Central Estonia aspires to be a region where people of all ages and backgrounds – young professionals, families and seniors – can thrive.** The region places a strong focus on ensuring access to quality social services. It seeks to provide good professional opportunities for all residents, including for seniors wishing to remain active in the workforce. Community involvement, social inclusion and support for newcomers are priorities.	**South Estonia imagines a region where people are healthy and able to live fulfilling lives.** The region wants to be attractive to young people, families, immigrants and retirees alike, offering high-quality education, strong community ties and a sense of belonging. The region hopes to foster pride in vocational paths for young people and offer opportunities for lifelong learning to help individuals adapt with the changing economy.
Environment and surroundings	**Central Estonia envisions well-connected, safe and vibrant communities with good infrastructure.** Central Estonia places an emphasis on creating high-quality, family-friendly living environments, with affordable rental housing options suited to young families and seniors.	**South Estonia wants to be a connected and liveable region.** South Estonia envisions green, affordable housing for residents and ready access to public services and sustainable transport. Residents and newcomers alike are meant to feel welcome and part of a cohesive community.
Business and economy	**Central Estonia is looking to diversify and modernise its regional economy.** The region wants to move beyond traditional sectors (like agriculture and forestry) by encouraging green entrepreneurship and support for SMEs. Workshop participants did not agree on one single industry of great potential for diversifying its economy, but saw potential in rural tourism, local foods, e-commerce and more. The region sees a future where access to financing for businesses – particularly for women, youth, and seniors – is expanded and where new businesses have access to good connectivity (transport and Internet) and a strong labour market.	**South Estonia wants a thriving, self-sustaining economy rooted in innovation.** It sees a future where local businesses, especially in sectors like biochemistry, forestry, food and renewable energy, are competitive and well-connected to universities and research centres. Entrepreneurship – particularly micro enterprises and youth-led ventures – is strongly encouraged. The region also wants to take advantage of its cultural heritage to attract visitors.

Source: OECD (2023[79]), "Foresight and vision setting workshops", Unpublished, OECD, Paris.

Regionals assets can be leveraged for development, including with the help of national policy levers

Central and South Estonia have distinct assets that can be leveraged – including using national policy tools – towards meeting their unique ambitions for regional development. Three groups of assets stood out as particularly important enablers during OECD interviews and workshops in these regions: i) building on education and skills assets to adapt the labour force and increase innovation; ii) leveraging culture and heritage assets to attract visitors and residents; and iii) building on quality-of-life assets to make each region a good place to live and work. The challenge for these two regions is to make the most out of their distinct assets in order to realise their ambitions for regional development. This section also highlights how the draft regional development agreements propose the national government tailor its policy levers in a place-based way to unlock the full potential of regional assets.

Building on education assets to adapt the labour force and increase innovation capacity

In Central Estonia, a responsive vocational education system is a notable source of support for development in the region. Central Estonia possesses a well-developed network of vocational institutions that serve both local and national labour market needs. These include the Järvamaa, Kehtna, Rakvere and

Viljandi[17] vocational schools, which offer programmes in areas as diverse as construction, food technology, and software development. Central Estonia does not have the highest enrolment rate in vocational education programmes: that distinction goes to North Estonia and South Estonia (see previous section). However, it has two of the counties with the highest proportion of students continuing their studies in vocational secondary education. In Järva county, 38% of students continue in vocational studies within a year after graduation, and Rapla county, 36% - both well above the national average of 25% (Haridussilm, 2025[80]). Participants in OECD interviews stressed that vocational education in Central Estonia is also distinguished by its responsiveness to industry needs. According to vocational education leaders, these schools work to adjust their offerings to meet regional needs, inviting enterprises to provide input on their curricula (OECD, 2024[81]).

Central Estonia's responsive vocational schools can contribute to its development ambitions by helping its labour force adapt to new demands. With their flexibility and strong local employer engagement, educational leaders feel that the vocational system in Central Estonia has the potential to reorient its offerings to train students and meet skill needs to support regional ambitions, such as an expansion of green business (OECD, 2024[81]). Building on this example, increasing green energy production (the region is interested in wind, solar, hydrogen and biogas) will require staff to develop, operate and maintain new energy infrastructure. Without access to people with sufficient skills in these areas, the region could face a skills bottleneck that constrains its ability to encourage new ventures in this sector (OECD, 2023[82]).

The Central Estonian pilot regional council has outlined how it would like the national government to adapt its policy levers to build on the region's vocational education asset, with an objective of making greater use of local entrepreneurs in vocational education (as well as basic education). Notably, it has asked the national vocational training agency to complete a survey and forecast of Central Estonian workforce skills. It has also asked the national Ministry of Education and Research to co-ordinate with vocational education institutions and the regional council to select specialisation areas for the schools to meet future workforce needs (Central Estonian Pilot Regional Council, 2024[83]). The agreement itself does not prescribe specialisation areas, leaving them up to the joint decision-making process between employers, vocational institutions and the regional council, but – as mentioned above – one example could be a specialisation in skills for the development, maintenance or operation of green energy infrastructure. This kind of partnership between regional actors and national ministries is an example of how the national government can use its tools to help a region take advantage of its vocational education asset to advance regional goals.

South Estonia's universities offer a strong foundation for knowledge creation and human capital development. The region benefits from the University of Tartu, the Estonian University of Life Sciences in Tartu and several other institutions of higher learning. The ready access to university education in South Estonia distinguishes the region from Central Estonia, which, apart from a branch of the University of Tartu dedicated to culture (discussed below), does not have any universities. Development specialists in the region note that the presence of universities provides South Estonia with strong human capital, which, combined with its well-educated and often entrepreneurial residents, creates good potential for innovation (OECD, 2024[81]). The research and development (R&D) functions of South Estonia's universities can also support regional innovation, if the region is able to leverage it. In South Estonia, this educational infrastructure can provide both new knowledge and human capital to support the region's ability to innovate (Uyarra, 2008[84]).

South Estonia's strong tertiary education supports the region's vision for innovation to thrive in strength areas. The region's desired futures emphasise innovation, envisioning, for example, smart specialisation strategies that are closely aligned with the region's strengths such as biochemistry, mechanics, forestry, food and biomass (OECD, 2023[79]). Innovation also has an important role to play in developing talent in the region. This point is emphasised in the draft South Estonian Regional Development Agreement, which proposes a range of actions to integrate education more closely with the local entrepreneurial landscape and to allow entrepreneurs to tap into research institutions to increase their innovation capacity (South Estonian Pilot Regional Council, 2024[85]).

South Estonia has ideas for how national policy levers can be used to capitalise on South Estonia's strong knowledge infrastructure. Its regional development agreement foresees that the national government – the Ministry of Economic Affairs and Communications and the Estonian Business and Innovation Agency – will work with South Estonian development organisations to support low-innovation but high-potential firms to innovate in products, processes and business models by connecting them with external consultants and regional research and education institutions. In addition, like Central Estonia, South Estonia sees a role for the national government in identifying and forecasting skills needs to connect academic pathways more directly to regional development goals (South Estonian Pilot Regional Council, 2024[85]).

Leveraging culture and heritage assets to attract residents and visitors

Central Estonia's cultural and heritage assets represent a notable development opportunity. The region is home to one of Estonia's two United Nations Educational, Scientific and Cultural Organization (UNESCO) World Heritage sites – one of the points of the Struve Geodetic Arc – and has a higher concentration of theatres, museums and tourism centres than most EU regions (OECD, 2024[86]). Viljandi, Estonia's "heritage capital" and a UNESCO Creative City of Crafts and Folk Art, stands out as a cultural hub in Estonia.[18] Viljandi is home to the University of Tartu's Viljandi Culture Academy, which specialises in heritage skills and creative entrepreneurship (OECD, 2024[81]). The academy works closely with local municipalities to equip students with entrepreneurial skills rooted in local culture. These assets create potential for the region to grow its visitor economy. But, despite these cultural assets, the region trails other Estonian and EU regions in international visitor numbers (OECD, 2024[86]).

South Estonia has leveraged its cultural assets as a driver for tourism. As described by one resident, the region has "strong identity, roots, [and] cultural heritage" (OECD, 2024[81]). The region ranks above OECD peers in the density of visitor centres, theatres, museums and galleries (OECD, 2024[86]). It has more entries in the UNESCO List of Intangible Cultural Heritage than any other region (four, including the smoke sauna of Võromaa and the polyphonic singing tradition of the Seto community) (UNESCO, 2024[87]). It has successfully positioned culture as a pillar of its regional marketing, for example in the Tartu 2024 European Capital of Culture initiative. This initiative brought together 22 municipalities in South Estonia to co-invest in cultural programming. This collaboration raised the region's profile nationally and internationally, attracting 7% more guests and 15% more foreign tourists compared to the same period the previous year (Visit Tartu, 2025[88]). South Estonia today attracts a relatively high share of overnight stays by foreign tourists and, although overall stays per capita remain just below the EU and OECD median, it is clear that culture is an asset that South Estonia is already putting to work (OECD, 2024[86]).

The cultural assets of both regions have a role to play in realising their development aspirations. Central Estonia's strengths in heritage skills and creative entrepreneurship provide a solid foundation for its development ambitions, which include creating a stronger regional brand that attracts investment, visitors and residents to the region. During OECD workshops in the region, participants considered that this brand should emphasise culture, building on Viljandi's reputation as a cultural hub (OECD, 2023[79]). It is important to note, however, that culture does not feature in the draft agreement for Central Estonia, in part because existing cultural assets are concentrated in just one county. In South Estonia, leveraging cultural assets is central to its hopes of attracting visitors. The region has taken significant steps to leverage culture for development in hosting Tartu 2024 European Capital of Culture and the region envisions building on the momentum from this event to raise regional visibility (OECD, 2023[79]).

Building on quality-of-life assets to make each region an attractive place to live and work

Quality of life is important for advancing regional development, making regions places where people want to live and work. Alongside economic performance, the quality of life in a region plays a critical role in attracting and retaining both residents and businesses. In Central and South Estonia, quality-of-life considerations emerged as central themes during stakeholder workshops. In particular, stakeholders identified affordable and adequate housing, work-life balance and satisfaction with the living environment as foundations for the regions' ambitions. These dimensions of well-being help define the everyday experience of residents and are integral to each region's attractiveness as a place for families and workers. This section explores how Central and South Estonia are thinking about these assets, the opportunities they present and the areas where targeted action is needed to fully unlock their potential.

Housing tends to be affordable in Central Estonia, but the housing stock needs a refresh to represent an asset. Affordable housing can be a major advantage in attracting both people and businesses to a region. In 2020, households in West Estonia spent the highest share of their income on housing costs (11.7%), followed by North Estonia (10.9%), South Estonia (10.6%) and Central Estonia (10.5%). Northeast Estonia recorded the lowest housing cost burden at 9.5%. In Central Estonia, residents also tend to live in larger dwellings, with nearly 2 rooms per person in 2021, compared to 1.6 in North Estonia (OECD, 2024[89]). Together, these figures suggest that a resident gets more for their housing money in Central Estonia. However, dwellings in the region to tend to be old: 47% of dwellings were built before 1970 (Central Estonia comes second only to West Estonia in the proportion of older dwellings) (Statistics Estonia, 2021[90]). They also tend to have fewer comfort characteristics than dwellings in other regions: the percentage of dwellings without water supply (21%), bathing facilities (13%), toilet facilities (24%) and central heating (57%) are highest in Central Estonia than any other region (Statistics Estonia, 2021[91]). Housing affordability is a driver of regional attractiveness for talent. Evidence from OECD countries, for example, shows that a 10-percentage-point increase in the share of the population satisfied with housing affordability can translate into a 1.8-percentage-point increase in the share of foreign-born working-age people in a region (OECD, 2023[92]). Without adequate quality housing, the region risks missing the opportunity to turn its affordability into a competitive advantage in attracting skilled workers and families.

Central Estonia considers that creating a more modern housing stock is essential to unlock the full potential of the region's affordability advantage. Central Estonia sees an important role for affordable living in its future, with stakeholders wanting the region to become a place for families to establish and thrive (OECD, 2023[79]). Affordable housing can also be an enabler for the goal of the Central Estonian draft agreement to develop entrepreneurship and attract a qualified workforce (Central Estonian Pilot Regional Council, 2024[83]). However, local stakeholders have expressed concern that the limited availability of quality dwellings could constrain growth: shortages of quality housing may deter new businesses and their employees from settling in the region. For this reason, the Central Estonian Pilot Council has set the "improvement of the quality of living spaces" as one of its objectives. Their agreement proposes, for example, expanding the dispersed settlement support programme, encouraging private housing development and developing "green villages" (sustainable private housing areas near businesses with all necessary infrastructure, such as utilities, roads, etc.). It also calls for clearer guidance and support for the small housing reconstruction support programme. In doing so, it invokes the help of the relevant ministries (including the Ministry of Regional Affairs and Agriculture, and the Ministry of Climate, which plays a role in construction and housing policy in Estonia) (Central Estonian Pilot Regional Council, 2024[83]).

Residents of Central and South Estonia emphasised their regions' advantages for family life and work-life balance compared to the capital region (OECD, 2024[81]; 2023[79]). Survey data from 2015 support this perception, with 77% of Central Estonian companies and just over 67% of South Estonian companies reporting that work-life balance was important in their workplaces, higher than in the capital region (at just under 67%) (Statistics Estonia, 2015[93]). When looking at actual working hours, South Estonia stands out more clearly: only 20% of enterprises in the region reported high overtime[19] among workers in 2021, and 46% reported no overtime at all, the highest share of zero overtime among the regions. These figures suggest a better work-life balance compared to North Estonia, where patterns align closely with the national average (22% high overtime, 43% no overtime) (Statistics Estonia, 2021[94]).

Residents of South Estonia report particularly high satisfaction with their living environment. Overall, 84% of residents in 2020 reported that they were satisfied with where they live, on par with the national average. What sets South Estonia apart, however, are high ratings across a range of quality-of-life indicators. Resident satisfaction with cultural leisure facilities is second only to North Estonia (nearly 73%, compared to nearly 74% in North Estonia). Residents were happy with their surroundings, including architecture (75%, compared to 73% in North Estonia) and public spaces like squares and parks (74%, second only to North Estonia at 75%). Residents also expressed strong satisfaction with outdoor air quality (87%, compared to a national average of 83%) and noise levels (85%, compared to 77% in North Estonia) (Statistics Estonia, 2020[95]). These results suggest that residents value South Estonia for its cultural amenities and its quiet, clean and attractive setting, which sets it apart from the capital region.

South Estonia sees its quality-of-life assets not only as a benefit to current residents but as a part of its value proposition to families, workers and students considering a move to the region. South Estonia envisions itself as a region where people of all walks of life can live healthy and fulfilling lives (OECD, 2023[79]). Its regional development agreement places strong emphasis on attracting and retaining new residents, with the goal of maintaining the population size in the region (South Estonian Pilot Regional Council, 2024[85]). This vision aligns closely with what residents already experience: high satisfaction with public spaces, clean air, low noise levels and cultural amenities, as well as a strong work-life balance, all of which can contribute to a healthier, quieter, more balanced way of life.

Conclusion: Place-based policy can help unlock regional assets and realise regional development ambitions

In both Central and South Estonia, regional assets provide a strong foundation for achieving development ambitions, but leveraging those assets to their fullest potential sometimes requires support from the national government. Each region has articulated ambitions for future development that are grounded in their own strengths. While this section does not present a comprehensive view of each region's strengths, it highlights three that were particularly prominent in OECD interviews and workshops: education, culture and quality-of-life assets. Yet both regions have also identified barriers – such as outdated housing stock in Central Estonia – that cannot be fully addressed through local action alone. The pilot development agreements present ideas of concrete ways national policy levers can be applied in a place-based way to help unlock the potential of these assets. This illustrates the potential of agreements – discussed further in Chapter 3 – as a way to align national policy tools with regional needs and assets to foster regional strengths.

Conclusion

This chapter shows differences in regional demographic, economic and well-being indicators alongside regional aspirations and assets across Estonia. For economic outcomes, the greatest and most persistent difference is that between the capital region and all other regions. While the capital region consistently outperforms others on many economic indicators, this chapter also shows that important differences exist among non-capital regions – differences that shape their challenges, assets and opportunities. The case studies of Central and South Estonia presented in this chapter also demonstrate that Estonian regions are distinct not only in their needs but by what they can offer, each with its own distinct assets and ambitions for development.

Together, differences in the needs and opportunities of the regions point to the relevance of a place-based approach to regional development that not only responds to regional disadvantages but also builds on local strengths and ambitions. The chapter provides a handful of examples of the national government adjusting its sector policy levers to meet the needs of Estonian regions (like providing targeted support encourage healthcare professionals to establish in underserved regions). It also contains examples of how regional development agreements foresee that the national government will apply its policy tools to leverage regional assets, such as targeted rental housing assistance in Central Estonia to overcome the limitations of its current housing stock. However, the next chapter shows that a place-based approach remains unfamiliar to much of the Estonian Government. Making this approach possible will require laying the institutional, governance and capacity foundations needed to support place-based policy.

References

Ahrend, R. et al. (2017), "What Makes Cities More Productive? Evidence on the Role of Urban Governance from Five OECD Countries", *OECD Regional Development Working Papers*, No. 2014/05, OECD Publishing, Paris, https://doi.org/10.1787/5jz432cf2d8p-en. [6]

Ahrend, R., A. Lembcke and A. Schumann (2017), "The role of urban agglomerations for economic and productivity growth", *International Productivity Monitor*, Vol. 32, pp. 161-179, https://ideas.repec.org/a/sls/ipmsls/v32y20179.html. [7]

Bodnár, K. and C. Nerlich (2022), "The macroeconomic and fiscal impact of population ageing", *Occasional Paper Series*, No. 296, European Central Bank, https://www.ecb.europa.eu/pub/pdf/scpops/ecb.op296~aaf209ffe5.en.pdf. [49]

Brezzi, M., L. Dijkstra and V. Ruiz (2011), "OECD Extended Regional Typology: The Economic Performance of Remote Rural Regions", *OECD Regional Development Working Papers*, No. 2011/6, OECD Publishing, Paris, https://doi.org/10.1787/5kg6z83tw7f4-en. [10]

Central Estonian Pilot Regional Council (2024), "Draft regional development agreement", Unpublished. [83]

CIA (2023), *Estonia*, Central Intelligence Agency, https://www.cia.gov/the-world-factbook/countries/estonia/#:~:text=After%20centuries%20of%20Danish%2C%20Swedish,collapse%20of%20the%20Soviet%20Union. (accessed on 24 January 2023). [12]

Dsiss, H. and M. Taru (2001), "Young students as a subject and resource of regional development (Õppurnoored kui regionaalse arengu subjekt ja ressurss)", https://www.sm.ee/sites/default/files/content-editors/Ministeerium_kontaktid/Uuringu_ja_analuusid/Sotsiaalvaldkond/oppurnoored_kui_regionaalse_arengu_subjekt_ja_ressurss.pdf. [70]

EC (2023), *2023 Country Report - Estonia*, European Commission, https://economy-finance.ec.europa.eu/system/files/2023-06/ip230_en.pdf. [27]

Eesti Pank (2024), *Labour Market Review 1/2024*, https://www.eestipank.ee/en/publications/labour-market-review/2024/labour-market-review-12024. [52]

EFGS (2018), *Estonia*, European Forum for Geography and Statistics, https://www.efgs.info/11-2-1-estonia/?utm_ (accessed on 22 April 2025). [76]

ERR (2024), "Estonian adults' skills well above OECD average", https://news.err.ee/1609547185/estonian-adults-skills-well-above-oecd-average. [64]

ERR (2024), "Tallinn continues to account for more than half of Estonia's GDP (Üle poole Eesti SKP-st annab jätkuvalt Tallinn)", ERR Majandus, https://www.err.ee/1609553299/ule-poole-eesti-skp-st-annab-jatkuvalt-tallinn. [1]

ERR (2024), "Tallinn still contributes over half of Estonia's GDP", https://news.err.ee/1609553356/tallinn-still-contributes-over-half-of-estonia-s-gdp. [29]

ERR (2023), "Harju County's contribution to Estonia's GDP declines slightly", https://news.err.ee/1609195783/harju-county-s-contribution-to-estonia-s-gdp-declines-slightly#:~:text=Last%20year%2C%2070%20percent%20of,contributions%20from%20industry%20and%20construction. [31]

Estonian Ministry of Economic Affairs and Communications (2020), "Transport and Mobility Development Plan 2021-2035", https://kliimaministeerium.ee/sites/default/files/documents/2023-09/Transpordi%20ja%20liikuvuse%20arengukava%202021-2035_EN%20%281%29.pdf. [77]

Estonian Ministry of Education and Research (2023), *PIAAC 2023 Adult skills in Estonia and Elsewhere in the World: Summary of Initial Results (PIAAC 2023 Täiskasvanute oskused Eestis ja mujal maailmas: esmaste tulemuste kokkuvõte)*, https://hm.ee/sites/default/files/documents/2024-12/L%C3%BChiraport_final_1.1.pdf. [63]

Estonian Ministry of Education and Research (2023), *Push and Pull Forces in the Teacher Labor Market - Literature Review (Õpetajate tööturu tõmbe- ja tõukejõud Kirjanduse ülevaade)*, https://www.hm.ee/sites/default/files/documents/2023-05/%C3%95petajate%20j%C3%A4relkasv.%20Kirjanduse%20%C3%BClevaade_0.pdf (accessed on 2025 April 22). [71]

Estonian Ministry of Education and Research (2020), *Teachers and School Leaders as Valued Professionals (Õpetajad ja koolijuhid väärtustatud professionaalidena)*, https://harno.ee/sites/default/files/documents/2021-02/TALIS2_kujundatud.pdf. [72]

Estonian Ministry of Finance (2021), *Regional Development Action Plan*. [18]

Estonian National Audit Office (2024), "Shortage of qualified teachers is greater than previously thought", https://www.riigikontroll.ee/Suhtedavalikkusega/Pressiteated/tabid/168/557GetPage/1/557Year/-1/ItemId/2429/amid/557/language/en-US/Default.aspx. [73]

Eurostat (2024), *Population on 1st January by Age, Sex, Type of Projection and NUTS 3 Region*, https://ec.europa.eu/eurostat/databrowser/view/proj_19rp3$defaultview/default/table. [19]

Eurostat (2023), *Gross Domestic Product (GDP) at Current Market Prices by NUTS 3 Region*, https://ec.europa.eu/eurostat/databrowser/view/nama_10r_3gdp$defaultview/default/table. [39]

Eurostat (2021), *Demographic Balances and Indicators by Type of Projection and NUTS 3 Region*, https://ec.europa.eu/eurostat/databrowser/bookmark/3fb67754-7209-460f-beba-71cc7adcee12?lang=en. [56]

Fadic, M. et al. (2019), "Classifying small (TL3) regions based on metropolitan population, low density and remoteness", *OECD Regional Development Working Papers*, No. 2019/06, OECD Publishing, Paris, https://doi.org/10.1787/b902cc00-en. [11]

Ferraro, S. and P. Kommer (2023), "Is there a labour market mismatch in Estonia? Measuring regional, occupational and industrial labour market mismatch", *Baltic Journal of Economics*, Vol. 23, pp. 200-228, https://doi.org/10.1080/1406099X.2023.2275865. [53]

Fina, S., B. Heider and M. Masso (2021), *Unequal Estonia*, Friedrich-Ebert-Stiftung, https://www.fes.de/politik-fuer-europa/unequal-estonia. [54]

Garcilazo, E. and J. Oliveira Martins (2013), "The Contribution of Regions to Aggregate Growth in the OECD", *OECD Regional Development Working Papers*, No. 2013/28, OECD Publishing, Paris, https://doi.org/10.1787/5k3tt0zzp932-en. [43]

Glaeser, E. and J. Gottlieb (2009), "The wealth of cities: Agglomeration economies and spatial equilibrium in the United States", *Journal of Economic Literature*, Vol. 47/4, pp. 983-1028, https://doi.org/10.1257/jel.47.4.983. [5]

Green, A. (2023), *When should place-based policies be used and at what scale?*, OECD-EC High-Level Workshop Series: Place-Based Policies for the Future, OECD, Paris, https://www.oecd.org/en/about/projects/place-based-policies-for-the-future.html. [57]

Haridussilm (2025), *Üldharidus: Lõpetajad (General education: Graduates)*, https://haridussilm.ee/ee/tasemeharidus/oppetasemed/yldharidus/lopetajad. [80]

Invest in Estonia (n.d.), *North Estonia*, https://investinestonia.com/regions/north-estonia/ (accessed on 26 March 2025). [30]

Invest in Estonia (n.d.), *South Estonia*, https://investinestonia.com/regions/south-estonia/ (accessed on 25 March 2025). [32]

Kalle, E. (2014), *Productivity evolution in Estonia (Tootlikkusealane evolutsioon eestis)*, https://digikogu.taltech.ee/et/item/07a9e2b8-568f-4f66-88fc-aa44a656b459. [99]

Leijen, Ä. et al. (2024), "The shortage of teachers in Estonia: Causes and suggestions for additional measures from the perspective of different stakeholders", *European Journal of Teacher Education*, Vol. 48/2, pp. 1-19, https://doi.org/10.1080/02619768.2024.2408641. [74]

Marshalian, M., P. Chan and M. Bournisien de Valmont (2023), "Networks and rural-urban linkages for rural innovation", *OECD Regional Development Papers*, No. 53, OECD Publishing, Paris, https://doi.org/10.1787/4928f26b-en. [8]

Mosiashvili, N. and J. Pareliussen (2020), "Digital technology adoption, productivity gains in adopting firms and sectoral spill-overs: Firm-level evidence from Estonia", *OECD Economics Department Working Papers*, No. 1638, OECD Publishing, Paris, https://doi.org/10.1787/ba9d00be-en. [36]

OECD (2025), *Educational Attainment - Regions*, OECD, Paris, http://data-explorer.oecd.org/s/1l0. [68]

OECD (2025), *Health Statistics - Regions*, OECD, Paris, http://data-explorer.oecd.org/s/1kz. [59]

OECD (2025), *Place-Based Policies for the Future*, OECD Publishing, Paris, https://doi.org/10.1787/e5ff6716-en. [3]

OECD (2024), "Estonia regional attractiveness analysis", Unpublished, OECD, Paris. [86]

OECD (2024), *Getting to Services in Towns and Villages: Preparing Regions for Demographic Change*, OECD Rural Studies, OECD Publishing, Paris, https://doi.org/10.1787/df1e9b88-en. [75]

OECD (2024), *Housing - Regions*, OECD, Paris, http://data-explorer.oecd.org/s/1md. [89]

OECD (2024), *OECD Economic Surveys: Estonia 2024*, OECD Publishing, Paris, https://doi.org/10.1787/33e6beee-en. [35]

OECD (2024), *OECD Focus Group Interviews*, Unpublished, OECD, Paris. [81]

OECD (2024), *OECD Regions and Cities at a Glance 2024*, OECD Publishing, Paris, https://doi.org/10.1787/f42db3bf-en. [66]

OECD (2024), *Population by 5-year age groups - Regions*, OECD,Paris, http://data-explorer.oecd.org/s/296. [17]

OECD (2024), *Population by Age and Sex - Cities and FUAs*, OECD, Paris, http://data-explorer.oecd.org/s/1mu. [9]

OECD (2023), *Assessing and Anticipating Skills for the Green Transition: Unlocking Talent for a Sustainable Future*, Getting Skills Right, OECD Publishing, Paris, https://doi.org/10.1787/28fa0bb5-en. [82]

OECD (2023), *Estonia: Adult skills (Survey of Adult Skills, PIAAC, 2023)*, OECD, Paris, https://gpseducation.oecd.org/CountryProfile?primaryCountry=EST&treshold=10&topic=AS (accessed on 22 April 2025). [62]

OECD (2023), "Foresight and vision setting workshops", Unpublished, OECD, Paris. [79]

OECD (2023), *OECD Regional Outlook 2023: The Longstanding Geography of Inequalities*, OECD Publishing, Paris, https://doi.org/10.1787/92cd40a0-en. [42]

OECD (2023), *Rethinking Regional Attractiveness in the New Global Environment*, OECD Regional Development Studies, OECD Publishing, Paris, https://doi.org/10.1787/a9448db4-en. [92]

OECD (2023), "Support materials - Country notes - Estonia", in *OECD Regions and Cities at a Glance 2022*, OECD Publishing, Paris, https://doi.org/10.1787/14108660-en. [50]

OECD (2022), *Employment by main economic activity - Regions*, http://data-explorer.oecd.org/s/2a7. [55]

OECD (2022), *Employment by Main Economic Activity - Regions*, OECD, Paris, http://data-explorer.oecd.org/s/1m2. [24]

OECD (2022), *Labour Productivity by Main Economic Activity - Regions*, OECD, Paris, http://data-explorer.oecd.org/s/1yx. [97]

OECD (2022), *OECD Regions and Cities at a Glance 2022*, OECD Publishing, Paris, https://doi.org/10.1787/14108660-en. [40]

OECD (2022), *Regions, Cities and Local Statistics*, OECD, Paris, https://www.oecd.org/en/topics/sub-issues/regions-cities-and-local-statistics.html (accessed on 5 September 2024). [41]

OECD (2022), *Shrinking Smartly in Estonia: Preparing Regions for Demographic Change*, OECD Rural Studies, OECD Publishing, Paris, https://doi.org/10.1787/77cfe25e-en. [16]

OECD (2021), *Improving the Provision of Active Labour Market Policies in Estonia*, Connecting People with Jobs, OECD Publishing, Paris, https://doi.org/10.1787/31f72c5b-en. [48]

OECD (2020), *Rural Well-being: Geography of Opportunities*, OECD Rural Studies, OECD Publishing, Paris, https://doi.org/10.1787/d25cef80-en. [47]

OECD (2020), *The Future of Regional Development and Public Investment in Wales, United Kingdom*, OECD Multi-level Governance Studies, OECD Publishing, Paris, https://doi.org/10.1787/e6f5201d-en. [45]

OECD (2018), "Rural 3.0: A Framework for Rural Development", *OECD Regional Development Papers*, No. 93, OECD Publishing, Paris, https://doi.org/10.1787/618f702b-en. [46]

OECD (2014), *How's Life in Your Region?: Measuring Regional and Local Well-being for Policy Making*, OECD Regional Development Studies, OECD Publishing, Paris, https://doi.org/10.1787/9789264217416-en. [58]

OECD (n.d.), *OECD Definition of Cities and Functional Urban Areas*, OECD, Paris, https://www.oecd.org/en/data/datasets/oecd-definition-of-cities-and-functional-urban-areas.html. [98]

OECD (n.d.), *OECD Economic Outlook Database*, OECD, Paris, https://www.oecd.org/en/topics/economic-outlook.html. [37]

OECD (n.d.), *OECD Geographical Definitions*, OECD, Paris, https://www.oecd.org/en/data/datasets/oecd-geographical-definitions.html. [4]

OECD/European Observatory on Health Systems and Policies (2023), *Estonia: Country Health Profile 2023*, State of Health in the EU, OECD Publishing, Paris, https://doi.org/10.1787/bc733713-en. [61]

Praxis (2020), "Adjustment of the economy and labor market of Ida - Viru County to the decline of the oil shale industry (Ida-Virumaa majanduse ja tööturu kohandamine põlevkivitööstuse vähenemisega)", https://www.praxis.ee/tood/ida-virumaa-polevkivitoostuse-vahenemine/. [28]

Russell, L., L. Yu and M. Andrews (2021), "Higher education and local educational attainment: Evidence from the establishment of U.S. colleges", *EdWorkingPaper*, No. 21-449, Annenberg Institute at Brown University, https://doi.org/10.26300/y9mc-gt63. [67]

Soe, R., M. Atiullah Saif and S. Agriesti (2022), "Framework for connecting the mobility challenges in low density areas to smart mobility solutions: The case study of Estonian municipalities", *European Transport Research Review*, Vol. 14/32, https://doi.org/10.1186/s12544-022-00557-y. [78]

South Estonian Pilot Regional Council (2024), "Draft regional development agreement", Unpublished. [85]

Statistics Estonia (2024), *HT551: Educational Institutions and Enrolment in Vocational Education by Indicator, County and Year*, https://andmed.stat.ee/en/stat/sotsiaalelu__haridus__kutseharidus/HT551/table/tableViewLayout2. [69]

Statistics Estonia (2024), *RV022U: Population by Sex, Age Group and County, 1 January*, https://andmed.stat.ee/en/stat/rahvastik rahvastikunaitajad-ja-koosseis rahvaarv-ja-rahvastiku-koosseis/RV022U. [15]

Statistics Estonia (2024), *TT4645: Labour Status of Population Aged 15-74 by Region, County and Age Group*, https://andmed.stat.ee/en/stat/sotsiaalelu tooturg tooturu-uldandmed aastastatistika/TT4645. [51]

Statistics Estonia (2023), *Population*, https://www.stat.ee/en/find-statistics/statistics-theme/population (accessed on 25 July 2024). [13]

Statistics Estonia (2023), *RAA0050: Gross Domestic Product (ESA 2010) by Year, County and Indicator*, https://andmed.stat.ee/en/stat/majandus rahvamajanduse-arvepidamine sisemajanduse-koguprodukt-(skp) regionaalne-sisemajanduse-koguprodukt/RAA0050/table/tableViewLayout2. [38]

Statistics Estonia (2023), *RAA0051: Gross Domestic Product by County and Economic Sector T (ESA 2010)*, https://andmed.stat.ee/en/stat/majandus rahvamajanduse-arvepidamine sisemajanduse-koguprodukt-(skp) regionaalne-sisemajanduse-koguprodukt/RAA0051/table/tableViewLayout2. [25]

Statistics Estonia (2023), *RV068: Population by Citizenship and Place of residence, 1 January*, https://andmed.stat.ee/en/stat/rahvastik rahvastikunaitajad-ja-koosseis rahvaarv-ja-rahvastiku-koosseis/RV068. [14]

Statistics Estonia (2023), *RVR02: Migration by Administrative Unit/Type of Settlement Region, Sex, and Type of Migration*, https://andmed.stat.ee/en/stat/rahvastik rahvastikusundmused ranne/RVR02. [21]

Statistics Estonia (2023), *TO001: Industrial Production by Economic Activity and County*, https://andmed.stat.ee/en/stat/majandus toostus/TO001/table/tableViewLayout2. [33]

Statistics Estonia (2023), *TU110: Capacity of Accommodation Establishments, Accommodated Tourists and Nights Spent by County*, https://andmed.stat.ee/en/stat/majandus turism-ja-majutus majutus/TU110/table/tableViewLayout2. [34]

Statistics Estonia (2022), "Households and dwellings in registers", https://www.stat.ee/sites/default/files/2022-05/Households%20and%20residences%20in%20registers.pdf. [96]

Statistics Estonia (2022), "Population census. Population has changed the least in Ida-Viru county, the most in Lääne county", https://www.stat.ee/en/news/native-and-immigrant-population-migration-31-december-2021. [20]

Statistics Estonia (2022), *TH753: Disability Free Life Expectancy by County, Sex and Age*, https://andmed.stat.ee/en/stat/sotsiaalelu tervishoid tervislik-seisund/TH753/table/tableViewLayout2. [60]

Statistics Estonia (2021), *RL21202: Buildings Containing Conventional Dwellings, Dwellings and Area of Dwellings, 31 December 2021 by Aasta, Asukoht, Ehitusaeg, Näitaja and Hoone tüüp*, http://andmed.stat.ee/en/stat/rahvaloendus rel2021 eluruumid/RL21202/table/tableViewLayout2. [90]

Statistics Estonia (2021), *RL21218: Area of Conventional Dwellings by Type of Building, Occupancy of Dwelling, Presence of Comfort Characteristics and Location (Administrative Unit), 31 December 2021*, https://andmed.stat.ee/en/stat/rahvaloendus__rel2021__eluruumid/RL21218/table/tableViewLayout2. [91]

Statistics Estonia (2021), *TKU10: Enterprises by Group of Enterprises and Share of Employees Who Have Worked Overtime During the Last 12 Months*, https://andmed.stat.ee/en/stat/sotsiaalelu__tooelukvaliteet__tooaeg/TKU10/table/tableViewLayout2. [94]

Statistics Estonia (2020), *KO11: Respondents by Year, Indicator, Sex, Type of Settlement/Administrative Unit, Satisfaction with Living Environment/Services and Assessment*, https://andmed.stat.ee/en/stat/eri-valdkondade-statistika__piirkondlik-rahulolu/KO11/table/tableViewLayout2. [95]

Statistics Estonia (2020), "The main driver of economic growth in 2019 was the service sector in Harju county", https://stat.ee/en/node/4557?utm (accessed on 25 March 2025). [26]

Statistics Estonia (2019), *PM1740: Production of Milk and Eggs by Year, Indicator, County and Quarter*, https://andmed.stat.ee/en/stat/Lepetatud_tabelid__Majandus.%20Arhiiv__Pellumajandus.%20Arhiiv/PM1740/table/tableViewLayout2. [22]

Statistics Estonia (2017), *PM040: Production of Field Crops by Country (2004–2017)*, https://andmed.stat.ee/en/stat/Lepetatud_tabelid__Majandus.%20Arhiiv__Pellumajandus.%20Arhiiv/PM040. [23]

Statistics Estonia (2015), *TKU68: Employers' Evaluation of the Importance to Combine Work and Family Life of Employees by Group of Enterprises (2009, 2015)*, https://andmed.stat.ee/et/stat/Lepetatud_tabelid__Sotsiaalelu.%20Arhiiv__Tooelukvaliteet.%20Arhiiv/TKU68. [93]

Study In Estonia (2024), *Universities*, https://www.studyinestonia.ee/study/universities. [65]

Suedekum, J. (2023), "The broadening of place-based policies – From reactive cohesion towards proactive support for all regions", OECD-EC High-Level Workshop Series: Place-Based Policies for the Future, OECD, Paris, https://www.oecd.org/content/dam/oecd/en/about/projects/cfe/place-based-policies-for-the-future/the-broadening-of-place-based%20policies-from-reactive-cohesion-towards-proactive-support-for-all-regions.pdf. [2]

Tsvetkova, A. et al. (2020), "The spatial dimension of productivity: Connecting the dots across industries, firms and places", *OECD Regional Development Working Papers*, No. 2020/01, OECD Publishing, Paris, https://doi.org/10.1787/ba5edb47-en. [44]

UNESCO (2024), *Estonia*, United Nations Educational, Scientific and Cultural Organization, https://ich.unesco.org/en/lists?text=&country[]=00070&multinational=3#tabs. [87]

Uyarra, E. (2008), "The impact of universities on regional innovation: A critique and policy implications", University of Manchester, https://research.manchester.ac.uk/en/publications/the-impact-of-universities-on-regional-innovation-a-critique-and- (accessed on 21 March 2025). [84]

Visit Tartu (2025), “The Year of the Capital of Culture brought many tourists to Tartu in the summer”, https://visittartu.com/the-year-of-the-capital-of-culture-brought-many-tourists-to-tartu-in-the-summer (accessed on 6 April 2025). [88]

Notes

[1] TL3 is the smaller scale at which the OECD Regional Database collects and publishes statistical indicators. In Europe, TL3 regions are consistent with the European Nomenclature of Territorial Units for Statistics third-level regions (NUTS 3) (Fadic et al., 2019[11]).

[2] It is also important to note, however, that it is not uncommon for individuals who live and work in one municipality to declare their residence in another, which can make obtaining accurate demographic figures challenging (OECD, 2022[16]). However, since 2022, the Estonian Government has applied a new index to more accurately gauge residence, drawing on multiple datasets to determine places of residence (e.g. looking at addresses in the Population Register, property ownership, electricity connections, education information, healthcare data, etc.) (Statistics Estonia, 2022[96]).

[3] A functional urban area (FUA) comprises a city and its commuting zone (OECD, n.d.[98]). It is considered metropolitan midsize if more than half of the population live in a FUA of 250 000 to 1.5 million inhabitants (OECD, 2023[42])

[4] With less than 15% of the region's population living in a rural place (OECD, n.d.[4]).

[5] Although care should be taken in considering data from before and after 2022, due to the introduction of a new index to gauge residence; see Endnote 2.

[6] The exception is Northeast Estonia, where net external migration briefly turned negative in 2020, probably driven by pandemic-related border restrictions. While all regions' net external migration dipped that year, Northeast Estonia was the only one to fall below zero.

[7] Of the 26 OECD countries with regional data (OECD, 2022[40]).

[8] USD per worker, constant prices, PPP converted.

[9] The difference in labour productivity between the capital region and the lowest-performing region (53%) may seem disproportionate to the difference in GDP per capita (which is nearly double). This may be, in part, due to differences between where people live and where they work. First, North Estonia has a relatively high number of commuters from other regions (Kalle, 2014[99]). It is the only region where the number of workers exceeds the number of employed residents (OECD, 2022[41]). The population figure may also be skewed by residents who are officially registered elsewhere for tax purposes (or by non-residents who have registered in Harju county).

[10] See endnote 9.

[11] In 2022, North Estonia had the highest productivity in the following sectors: construction; wholesale and retail trade; repair of motor vehicles and motorcycles; transportation and storage; accommodation and food

service activities; information and communication; financial and insurance activities; professional, scientific and technical activities; administrative and support service activities; public administration, defence, education, human health and social work activities; arts, entertainment and recreation; other service activities; activities of household and extra-territorial organisations and bodies. Other regions lead in: agriculture, forestry and fishing (Northeast Estonia); industry excluding construction (Northeast Estonia); manufacturing (Northeast Estonia); and real estate activities (South Estonia) (OECD, 2022[97]).

[12] With the lowest labour productivity in: agriculture, forestry and fishing; industry (except construction); manufacturing; wholesale and retail trade; repair of motor vehicles and motorcycles; transportation and storage; accommodation and food service activities; trade, transport, and tourism; arts, entertainment and other services.

[13] This index is based on the matching function, which predicts the number of hires or new job matches each quarter based on the number of unemployed individuals and the number of job vacancies. Any variation in hiring that cannot be explained by unemployment and vacancies is attributed to differences in matching efficiency (Ferraro and Kommer, 2023[53]).

[14] The Estonian Academy of Arts, the Estonian Academy of Music and Theatre, the Estonian Business School, the Estonian Entrepreneurship University of Applied Sciences, Tallinn Health Care College, Tallinn University, Tallinn University of Technology (TalTech), the Estonian Academy of Security Sciences, TTK University of Applied Sciences, the Estonian Free Church Theological Seminary and the Institute of Theology of the Estonian Evangelical Lutheran Church.

[15] University of Tartu, Estonian University of Life Sciences, Tartu Applied Health Sciences University, Pallas University of Applied Sciences, The Estonian Military Academy, and the Estonian Aviation Academy

[16] Northeast Estonia has a TalTech campus and West Estonia has a college of the University of Tartu in Pärnu.

[17] While Viljandi is a part of the South Estonia NUTS3 region, it opted to be a part of the Central Estonia pilot regional council for the purpose of the preparation of the regional development agreements (Chapter 3). Because this section focuses on these pilot regions, Viljandi is considered a part of Central Estonia.

[18] Here again, Viljandi is considered within the Central Estonia pilot region (see endnote 17).

[19] Meaning more than a fifth of their employees worked overtime in the past year.

2 Laying the foundations for place-based regional development in Estonia

This chapter focuses on the opportunities for the Estonian Government to more fully embrace a place-based approach to regional development. It explores how, on the national level, enhancing cross-ministry working and introducing greater place sensitivity in sector policy making can better equip the government to address multi-dimensional regional development challenges. It also considers how the national government can help municipalities participate more fully in a place-based approach, including by addressing capacity gaps and providing new pathways for national and subnational planning processes to be complementary and mutually enforcing. The government's ability to realise these opportunities comes down to capacity and incentives, ensuring that all relevant actors have the resources and skills to participate and the motivation to work together. The chapter examines how Estonia can build capacity and establish incentives to support a more place-based approach.

Introduction

While Chapter 1 builds a case for place-based policy for regional development in Estonia, Estonia is missing three prerequisites to pursuing this approach (Table 2.1). The first is that place-based policy must be intentionally spatially targeted. This is rare in Estonia: while the Estonian Government focuses on regional development driven by sector policies, the fact that sector policy tends to be spatially blind limits line ministries from tailoring interventions to regional and local needs. The second prerequisite is that the different parts of the government must be able to work together for regional development, taking a cross-cutting approach to address multi-dimensional regional development challenges that transcend individual policy areas. In Estonia, national policy is not only spatially blind but also tends to operate without a strong connection to the Ministry of Regional Affairs and Agriculture, the ministry with a mandate for advancing regional development. The third prerequisite is the capacity for place-sensitive policy design and implementation taking into account the needs and opportunities of places when designing national policies. In Estonia, opportunities remain to better align national and local planning and policy making to leverage regional tools and opportunities for development (such as those identified in Chapter 1). Without these three foundations in place, Estonia's ability to take a place-based approach for regional development remains limited.

This chapter explores each of the three prerequisites, offering recommendations for how to lay these foundations. To enable a place-based approach to regional development, the Estonian Government can focus on building capacity and creating clear incentives for doing so on the national and subnational levels. On the national level, this means that the Ministry of Regional Affairs and Agriculture, with the support of the centre of government, sets incentives for line ministries to take a co-ordinated, cross-sector approach for regional development, and supports this with strong institutional processes. On the subnational level, building capacity for planning, implementation and investment can help put local authorities in the driver's seat for regional development efforts. Capacity building is particularly important in three areas: strategic planning, spending and investment and stakeholder engagement. At the same time, bridging the national-local divide requires that Estonia make dialogue and aligning planning processes among levels of government systematic.

Table 2.1. Three missing prerequisites for place-based policy for regional development

Prerequisites for place-based policy for regional development	How Estonia reflects – or does not reflect – these prerequisites
Intentionally spatially targeted policy Tailors policy tools – resources, government intervention – to specific places within the country.	**Mostly spatially blind policy** Sectoral policy on the national level is mostly spatially blind. Intentionally spatially targeted policy focuses on two regions.
Policy designed to respond to multi-dimensional regional development challenges Requires a cross-cutting approach to address complex, multi-dimensional regional development challenges, aligning different sectors to take advantage of complementarities and guard against spillover effects.	**Sectoral silos hinder a multi-dimensional approach** Weak links between sectoral ministries and the Ministry of Regional Affairs and Agriculture limit the government's ability to respond to multi-dimensional regional development challenges.
Place-sensitivity to regional conditions and opportunities Builds an understanding of regional context, conditions and opportunities to design policy that drives regional development.	**Gaps in vertical co-ordination and capacity limit tailoring to regional needs and opportunities** A disconnect in strategy setting between the national and local levels means that bottom-up input does not usually contribute to national strategy. In addition, local governments face capacity constraints that limit their own ability to plan for and act on regional challenges and opportunities.

Sources: Adapted from OECD (2020[1]), *Regional Policy for Greece Post-2020*, https://doi.org/10.1787/cedf09a5-en and OECD (2025[2]), *Place-Based Policies for the Future*, OECD Publishing, Paris, based on Estonian Ministry of Regional Affairs and Agriculture (2023[3]), *Regional Development and Policy*, https://www.agri.ee/en/regional-development-and-policy; Estonian Government (2021[4]), *Regional Policy Program 2021-2024 [Regionaalpoliitika programm 2021-2024]*, https://www.fin.ee/media/2654/download; OECD (2023[5]), "Questionnaire completed by the Estonian Ministry of Regional Affairs and Agriculture", OECD, Paris.

Driving a co-ordinated regional approach across the national government

For place-based policy to flourish in Estonia, interventions must be tailored to regional needs and sectors must work together to drive regional development – two of the prerequisites introduced above. In practice, however, line ministries tend to take a spatially blind approach[1] to strategy setting and policy making, without working closely with the Ministry of Regional Affairs and Agriculture to integrate a regional perspective into their work. This persists despite the ambitions of Estonia's national development strategy Estonia 2035 which promotes a cross-sectoral approach – often with a regional dimension – to implementing national objectives. However, there is a gap between the intention of the strategy and the reality of its implementation, with ministries reverting to a sectoral approach to take it forward. In addition, there are few arrangements that help to facilitate cross-government working to support regional development in Estonia. Ultimately, a sector-focused and spatially blind approach can limit Estonian ministries' ability to tackle complex and multi-dimensional regional development challenges.

This section is dedicated to how the Estonian Government can take a more co-ordinated regional approach across the national government. It discusses the barriers to cross-government working that is sensitive to regional needs and opportunities, focusing on misaligned incentives as a key challenge. It provides recommendations for how Estonia can overcome this challenge, including by creating regular opportunities for ministries to come together to consider regional issues, strengthening regional impact assessments and developing financial incentives that encourage joint working.

Sector policy tends to be spatially blind in Estonia

This sub-section examines how a predominantly spatially blind approach to planning and policy limits ministries' ability to positively influence regional development. Even though ministries are asked to complete regional impact assessments for new strategies or legal texts, sector strategy and policy do not generally consider regional challenges and opportunities. However, when line ministries default to a spatially blind approach, their plans and policies may be less effective in promoting balanced regional development. The sub-section ends with recommendations for how to strengthen the role of regional impact assessments as a tool to encourage line ministries to consider how their plans and policies affect regions.

Countries take different approaches to organising government action to meet regional development objectives. One approach hinges on a comprehensive national regional development policy that sets a clear direction to guide regional interventions within sector policies. Another focuses on well-coordinated sector policies that promote specific sectoral goals while also supporting regional development (OECD, 2020[6]). Estonia takes the latter approach. Following in the tradition of its first regional strategy (Box 2.1), which emphasised the "purposeful linking of sectoral policies with the objectives of regional development" (Estonian Government, 1999[7]), the Estonian Government has framed sector policy as a force to shape and drive regional development. Taking this approach requires strong cross-sector co-ordination to help find alignment and complementarities among individual sector policies strategies and regional development objectives (OECD, 2024[8]). The Estonian Regional Policy Action Plan recognises this, stating "without the participation of sectoral policies and effective co-operation, achieving the country's comprehensive regional development goals is not realistic" (Estonian Ministry of Finance, 2021[9]).

Box 2.1. A brief history of regional development policy in Estonia

Over the past decades, the Estonian Government has increasingly recognised the importance of regional and local initiative and potential in improving development outcomes across the country, at least in principle.

Following independence in 1991, Estonia's approach to regional development, dubbed a "passive regional policy paradigm", relied on market forces to drive regional development rather than direct intervention. It downplayed the roles of regions in policy making by using centralised decision making and top-down implementation.

Starting in the mid-1990s, policy makers began to pivot towards a more active approach that considered how to harness the endogenous potential of regions. The 1994 Regional Policy Concept marked a symbolic shift from a passive to a more active approach to promoting regional development. The Estonian Government formulated this concept against a backdrop of uncertainty generated by transitioning to a market economy and the impact this could have on regions. In addition, the government had limited state funding for regional initiatives. Given these constraints, the Regional Policy Concept represented a "light touch" approach to regional development. For example, it specified that any "regional economic incentives [from the national government] are, as a rule, viewed as temporary measures to strengthen or restore local coping capacity."

Estonia's first regional development strategy in 1999 advanced the regional approach further. Funding for regional development had grown and a suite of development strategies were prepared on the national and subnational levels (including the Estonian Economic Development Plan 1998-2002, the Estonia 2010 national plan and development plans for all counties). With these enablers in place, the strategy was able to be more ambitious and concrete than the first concept. For example, it tried to strengthen the focus on local initiatives introduced in the 1994 Regional Policy Concept by ensuring adequate resources for county development activities and focusing on increasing the innovation capacity of all the regions.

With the prospect of European Union (EU) accession on the horizon, Estonia introduced a diverse array of regional programmes, focusing on small island development, industrial areas, agricultural regions, central networks, local initiatives and cross-border co-operation. Estonia's accession to the European Union in 2004 brought with it a series of reforms that supported regional development policy influenced by EU standards. These included the development of local governance and financing systems, improving public services to comply with EU requirements and building EU statistical standards for administrative units.

Sources: Sootla, G. and K. Kattai (2018[10]), "Institutionalization of subnational governance in Estonia: European impacts and domestic adaptations", https://doi.org/10.1080/13597566.2018.1511979; Estonian Ministry of Regional Affairs and Agriculture (2023[3]), *Regional Development and Policy*, https://www.agri.ee/en/regional-development-and-policy; OECD (2023[5]), "Questionnaire completed by the Estonian Ministry of Regional Affairs and Agriculture", OECD, Paris; CoR (n.d.[11]), *Division of Powers - Estonia*, https://portal.cor.europa.eu/divisionpowers/Pages/Estonia-Introduction.aspx; Estonian Government (1999[7]), *Estonian Regional Development Strategy (Approved by the Government of the Republic of Estonia on November 16, 1999, Agenda Item No. 24)*, https://web.archive.org/web/20140513132451/http://www.siseministeerium.ee/failid/reg_strateegia.rtf, Estonian Government (1994[12]), *Regional Policy Concept*, https://www.riigiteataja.ee/akt/30494.

In reality, sector strategies and their associated policies tend to be largely spatially blind (Loewen, 2018[13]; Estonian Ministry of Regional Affairs and Agriculture, n.d.[14]). This begins when ministries set their own strategies. Estonia 2035 encourages ministries to adopt a regional lens – i.e. taking into consideration the impact of a strategy and its implementation on a region, and/or adjusting to regional needs and capacities – and foresees collaboration among leading line ministers and the Minister of Regional Affairs and

Agriculture to achieve goals related to regional development (Table 2.2). However, this does not always extend to its implementation. National civil servants note that Estonia 2035 is primarily implemented through specific strategies and programmes, mostly managed by the originating line ministry. For example, the Estonian Ministry of Education and Research takes forward relevant parts of Estonia 2035 through its own strategy – the Education Strategy 2021-2035 – and related programming (Estonian Ministry of Education and Research, 2021[15]).[2] This ultimately reinforces a sector-driven focus to regional-level policy or programming interventions (OECD, 2024[16]). Indeed, the sector strategies that advance Estonia 2035 do not tend have a strong regional dimension (OECD, 2024[16]). Take the example of Estonia's transport plan: it acknowledges urban and rural challenges and the importance of connecting urban and rural areas, but otherwise has a strong national spin. It contains mostly national-level quantitative monitoring indicators, aside from a handful of targets related to – for example – urban areas and specific airport developments (Estonian Ministry of Economic Affairs and Communications, 2020[17]).

The predominant "one Estonia" approach to sector policy has two main motivations. For some, a "one Estonia" approach is rooted in the belief that Estonia – with its population of 1.3 million inhabitants – is small enough to be treated as a relatively homogenous territory. Others may believe that a regional approach adds complexity and costs to policy making, as it requires collecting regional data and engaging with many actors across all regions (OECD, 2024[16]). Some may be motivated by a combination of both views.

Table 2.2. Estonia 2035 frames sectoral activities as primary contributors to regional development goals

Selected examples of activities related to regional development outlined in Estonia 2035

Area of change	Activities	Leading ministers	Other responsible ministers
Skills and the labour market	Designing a harmonised upper secondary education system	Education	**Regional Affairs**
	Reorganising the network of upper secondary schools and basic schools in co-operation with local governments and empowering them in reviewing and reorganising the basic education network		
	Supporting the labour markets in Northeast and Southeast Estonia[3] to ensure a regional balance	Economic Affairs; **Regional Affairs**	Social Affairs; Climate; Education
	Providing higher education in regional colleges and expanding their functions, taking into account regional policy objectives	Education	**Regional Affairs**
Sustainability of the nation, health and social protection	Developing cross-sectoral and community-based integrated prevention and counselling services to improve the awareness of people, change their attitudes and behaviour, and prevent deaths due to accidents and injuries	Health; Interior	Culture; Education; Climate; **Regional Affairs**; Justice; Economic Affairs
	Shaping a living environment that supports health	Climate; **Regional Affairs**; Health	Education
	Developing needs-based social protection	Social Affairs; Economic Affairs	Culture; **Regional Affairs**;
	Developing care services	Social Affairs	**Regional Affairs**; Interior; Education
Economy and climate	Launching a package of services in the county of Ida-Viru to support the exit from oil shale energy	**Regional Affairs**	Economic Affairs; Climate; Culture; Education; Social Affairs
	Ensuring research and development (R&D) co-operation between R&D institutions and enterprises in focus areas important to the economy of Estonia and its regions	Economic Affairs; Education	Climate; **Regional Affairs**, Finance
	Developing the regional business environment in co-operation with local governments	**Regional Affairs**	Economic Affairs; Education, Climate

Area of change	Activities	Leading ministers	Other responsible ministers
Space and mobility	Increasing the regional accessibility of cultural areas to ensure a more attractive living environment also outside the centres of attraction and to support the cohesion of society and well-being of people	Culture	**Regional Affairs**; Education; Economic Affairs; Climate
	Continuously implementing solutions that contribute to the green transition and supportive planning in co-operation with local governments to mitigate, reduce the effect of and adapt to climate change	**Regional Affairs**; Climate	Economic Affairs
	Developing a sustainable waste management and public water supply as well as sewerage infrastructure and services in co-operation with local governments	Climate	**Regional Affairs**
Regional development	Organising the regulatory framework for strategic planning (at the national, local and regional levels) and for preparing the national budget	Secretary of State; Finance	**Regional Affairs**
	Reducing regional inequalities and strengthening the administrative and development capacity of local governments	**Regional Affairs**	Economic Affairs; Education; Social Affairs; Health; Culture; Climate
	Building the capacity of local governments and the community as partners of the state in creating a safe living environment and improving crisis preparedness	Defence; Secretary of State; Interior	Justice; Economic Affairs; **Regional Affairs**; Climate

Note: "Education" refers to the Minister of Education and Research, "Economic Affairs" to the Minister of Economic Affairs and Information Technology, "Regional Affairs" to the Ministry of Regional Affairs and Agriculture.
Source: Estonian Government (2023[18]), *Estonia 2035: Action Plan of the Government of the Republic (11 May 2023)*, https://valitsus.ee/media/6506/download.

Recognising sectoral policy as a key driver of regional development is one thing; ensuring its impact aligns with regional needs is another. Successfully using sectoral policy as an instrument for regional development requires understanding its potential regional impacts (Ferry, 2021[19]). With this in mind, the Estonian Government also tries to encourage line ministries to systematically review regional impacts as part of their impact assessment protocol. This represents a rules-based co-ordination mechanism to complement Estonia 2035's strategy-based co-ordination. Together, the two tools should (in theory) encourage ministries to adopt a regional lens when they are planning and when they are creating legal acts to further their objectives. Despite provisions and guidelines for considering regional impacts in new laws and policies (Box 2.2), however, regional impact assessment is weak in practice. Stakeholders report that the requirement to consider the regional impact of new laws and strategies is too often treated as a "check-the-box" exercise by line ministries, with limited impact on decision making (OECD, 2023[5]; 2024[16]).

Box 2.2. Regional development and Estonia's Rules for Good Legislative and Regulatory Process

Regional development is one of the six key impact areas highlighted in Estonia's Rules for Good Legislative and Regulatory Process for evaluators to consider. The accompanying impact assessment checklist provides greater detail on what the Estonian Government considers good practice for evaluating regional impacts: it asks for evaluators to consider, for example, whether a policy or measure has different effects across regions related to access to services, economic opportunities and spatial development. It also asks evaluators to consider whether the proposed approach may widen or reduce interregional disparities and how it affects the capacity of local actors to participate in policy making and regional development.

Source: Estonian Ministry of Justice and Digital Affairs (n.d.[20]), *Impact assessment of legislative acts*, https://www.justdigi.ee/oigusloome-arendamine/hea-oigusloome-ja-normitehnika/oigustloovate-aktide-mojude-hindamine.

Relying in large part on spatially blind policies to drive balanced development, as Estonia is in effect doing, comes with some risks. They can contain a hidden urban bias and fail to address local market conditions and spillovers, ultimately having different impact in different regions (OECD, 2011[21]). In Estonia, some sectoral policies that do not account for regional differences have been found to work against the objectives of regional and rural policy measures. The implementation of these spatially blind policies is sometimes concentrated in already rapidly developing growth centres, such as Tallinn and Tartu (Kattai et al., 2020[22]). The Estonian Government, for example, points to the urban concentration of sector support measures,[4] a long list that includes expanding labour market services to new target groups and providing new labour market services, organising the school network and modernising schools, and developing health centres in tourist areas. Only 20% of this support targeting businesses and 40% of the measures aimed at infrastructure development have reached beyond the counties of Harju and Tartu (those surrounding Tallinn and Tartu) (Estonian Ministry of Finance, 2019[23]). As a result, instead of fostering balanced development, spatially blind policies may exacerbate existing regional inequalities, contradicting Estonia's goals for balanced growth.

Line ministries have something to gain from thinking regionally, too: the possibility of better outcomes in their sectors. Different regions have unique challenges, strengths and opportunities; sector policies that are sensitive to regions can enhance policy effectiveness. Take the example of healthcare, where regional approaches support national governments' efforts to address healthcare workforce shortages. Significant inequalities in the distribution of healthcare staff among regions have prompted many countries to put in place programmes encouraging or requiring healthcare staff to work in underserved areas. France, for example, offers financial support for doctors to set up their practices in so called "medical deserts" (OECD, 2021[24]). In short, by tailoring their approaches to take into account regional needs and opportunities, sector ministries can contribute to meeting their own policy objectives.

The Estonian Government can favour sector policy that is sensitive to regional impacts by encouraging a more meaningful regional impact assessment. External accountability measures can build ministry commitment to strong regional impact assessments. One option for external accountability is to display a "regional impact dashboard" on the Ministry of Regional Affairs and Agriculture's website that shows all of the different regional impacts of proposed laws and strategies. The Estonian Government can also signal that it is serious about this requirement by making it clear that failing to consider regional impacts could be considered grounds for corrective measures (OECD, 2020[25]). While this is an action for a different part of government than the Ministry of Regional Affairs and Agriculture – one with the authority to make pronouncements about regulatory policy or legislative process, such as the Ministry of Justice or the Government Office – doing so creates an additional incentive for ministries to carry out the impact assessment and to do it well.[5]

Finally, capacity building has a role to play in ensuring strong regional impact assessment. To build the necessary skills and ensure that those conducting the assessments have the data that they need, the Estonian Government could provide specific guidance and training on regional impact assessment for the civil servants in each ministry that produce such reports (Box 2.3). These learning materials could, for example, provide information about regional data, templates or lists of what to include and examples of strong regional impact assessments.

Box 2.3. Northern Ireland in the United Kingdom promotes high-quality assessment of policy impact on rural areas

Northern Ireland's Rural Needs Act (2016) requires public authorities to "have due regard to rural needs" when developing, implementing or revising policies, strategies and services. Public authorities can complete a Rural Needs Impact Assessment to help them fulfil the requirement, although following the template for this assessment is not strictly necessary if public authorities can still show that they have fulfilled their "due regard duty".

The Department of Agriculture, Environment and Rural Affairs (DAERA) supports civil servants in producing meaningful rural impact assessments by providing guidance materials and training. It also provides a template. While DAERA does not have a role in assuring the quality of these assessments, it does play a role in opening the assessments to additional scrutiny. Public authorities must report on how they have paid due regard to rural needs in their annual reports and DAERA compiles these reports to show how rural needs have been addressed across public bodies to lay before Northern Ireland's legislature.

Sources: DAERA (2018[26]), *A Guide to the Rural Needs Act (Northern Ireland) 2016 for Public Authorities (Revised)*, https://www.daera-ni.gov.uk/publications/guide-rural-needs-act-northern-ireland-2016-public-authorities-revised; Bryce, B. (2024[27]), "Rural Proofing: Lessons from OECD countries and potential application to health", https://doi.org/10.1787/4011899a-en; Shortall, S. and E. Sherry (2019[28]), *Rural Proofing in Northern Ireland: An Overview and Recommendations on Guidance, Implementation and Governance*, https://www.afbini.gov.uk/publications/rural-proofing-northern-ireland-overview-and-recommendations.

There are few arrangements that help to facilitate cross-government collaboration for regional development in Estonia

This section discusses how Estonia's existing cross-government co-ordination mechanisms lack a strong focus on aligning national policies with regional needs. None of the Estonian Government's co-ordination mechanisms, including its national Regional Development Action Plan, systematically promote cross-sector consideration of regional development. This gives little reason for line ministries to work together to improve regional development outcomes. Without this type of inter-ministerial co-ordination, the Estonian Government may struggle to tackle the interconnected challenges of regional development. This section presents recommendations for strengthening co-ordination for regional development, including by introducing new formal agreements between ministries and introducing a regional perspective to existing fora for cross-sector collaboration.

The Estonian Government introduced a Regional Development Action Plan in 2021, administered by the Ministry of Regional Affairs and Agriculture, with the intention of co-ordinating activities across government in support of balanced territorial development (Estonian Ministry of Regional Affairs and Agriculture, 2024[29]). To date, the plan has been used primarily as a monitoring tool. The most recent monitoring report, for example, observes how ministries' policies contribute to regional development but does not issue targeted recommendations or binding requirements for how ministries should improve their contributions. The plan states that line ministries are expected to consider the monitoring review when developing their own plans and policies (Estonian Ministry of Regional Affairs and Agriculture, 2024[30]). However, a lack of concrete guidance for how to do so, along with few incentives to take the guidance onboard, may limit its impact on shaping sector policy.

Steering committees and the Government Office serve as champions for co-ordination across ministries, but regional development remains largely outside the scope of their efforts. A primary tool for co-ordination across the Estonian Government is steering committees, created and maintained by line ministries to engage with each other in specific areas (OECD, 2024[16]; Estonian Government, 2021[31]). These are often devoted to strategy implementation: there is, for example, a steering committee to support the Culture Development Plan 2021-2030, which includes representatives from a wide range of ministries[6] (Estonian Ministry of Culture, 2021[32]). The Government Office is also viewed as a facilitator of cross-government co-ordination, with a special strategy unit dedicated to co-ordinating and monitoring activities related to Estonia 2035 (SGI, 2024[33]).[7] None of these co-ordination tools serve to "connect the dots" for regional development, however, leaving ministries to continue to pursue their own sector-specific goals with little consideration for regional development.

Among Estonia's various inter-ministerial co-ordination mechanisms, the Economic Cabinet stands out as a high-level co-ordination mechanism with great relevance to regional development. It is the newest addition to Estonia's inter-ministerial co-ordination structures, established in 2024 to bring together cabinet members to discuss economic and security issues every two weeks (ERR, 2024[34]). However, the cabinet currently does not have a strong regional focus, despite the Ministry of Regional Affairs and Agriculture's interest in bringing a regional perspective to the cabinet by inviting representatives of the pilot regional councils (Chapter 3) to meetings.

The fact that Estonia's cross-government co-ordination tools do not have a strong regional development focus limits the ability of the Estonian Government to work together to address multi-dimensional regional development issues. These issues require a co-ordinated approach to ensure policies are coherent and, ideally, complementary and prevent negative spillover effects. Empirical research on the country level suggests that co-ordinating policies can help maximise development outcomes (Braga de Macedo, Oliveira Martins and Rocha, 2014[35]). Evidence suggests the same may apply on the regional level. In a study of 23 regions, poorer regions successfully converging with their peers had a formula: parallel improvements in horizontal co-ordination of policies, infrastructure, human capital and regional institutional capacity (OECD, 2012[36]). Without a co-ordinated approach to help ensure that policies are aligned and mutually reinforcing, policy makers risk unintended spillover effects. For example, research shows that improving transport alone can backfire: if there are no local jobs, better connectivity simply makes it easier for people to leave the region (OECD, 2012[36]).

One way Estonia can improve cross-sectoral co-ordination and collaboration is by expanding the use of agreements to make explicit how ministries will work together for regional development. It can do so by: i) making the most of the existing pilot development agreements that focus on two Estonian regions; and ii) considering creating new contracts to formalise working relationships across government. These two options are described below:

- Ministries can create a co-ordinated action plan outlining how they will work together to fulfil their commitments in pilot regional development agreements (Chapter 3). Many of these commitments already entail collaboration among signatory ministries. For example, an action in the Central Estonian Regional Development Agreement for the Ministries of Climate and of Economic Affairs and Communications is to create favourable terms for electrical connections for start-ups establishing in the region, in collaboration with local governments (Central Estonian Pilot Regional Council, 2024[37]). A cross-government action plan will help make concrete how ministries will work together to fulfil these commitments.
- Ministries can also consider entering into other contracts with their peers to advance regional development objectives. For example, the Ministry of Regional Affairs and Agriculture could propose using a contract to make explicit how the ministries invoked in the Estonia 2035 objectives relevant to regional development (Table 2.2) will work together to implement the objectives.

The government can also create regular opportunities for ministries to come together and "connect the dots" for regional development. There is no official regional policy council, advisory group or other such institution at the national level to convene line ministries in order to collaborate on the design and implementation of regional policy. The Ministry of Regional Affairs and Agriculture has already proposed that regional development topics be discussed regularly in the Economic Cabinet. This arrangement would give regional development policy greater prominence and set the foundation for more active, regular co-ordination. Italy's cross-ministerial committee for its National Strategy for Inner Areas (Box 2.5) provides an example of inter-ministerial co-ordination and collaboration at the highest level. Regional development co-ordination and collaboration can also benefit from dialogue at the civil servant level, as in Sweden (Box 2.4). To this end, the ministry could consider developing its own steering committee for regional development. This option may require more resources and time but is a way to make space for cross-sector co-ordination that is within the power of the ministry.

Alternatively, the ministry could focus on advocating for adjustments to existing steering committees in order to create space for discussion specifically related to regional development (OECD, 2025[38]). It could, for example, advocate that a meeting of relevant steering committees (e.g. the steering committees for Estonia 2035, for the Education Strategy, for the Transport and Mobility Strategy) periodically be dedicated to the regional impacts of the activities under the steering committees' purview, facilitated by the Ministry of Regional Affairs and Agriculture. Making space for discussion focused on regions requires that the members of the steering groups – generally from several ministries across government – apply a regional lens.

Box 2.4. A co-ordination platform for the political and operational sides of regional development in Sweden

In Sweden, it is the job of regional development policy makers to convince other ministries that they should adopt a territorial lens when planning and designing sector policies. The Forum for Sustainable Regional Development 2022-2030 – part of the implementation plan for the National Strategy for Sustainable Regional Development throughout Sweden 2021-2030 – is one important co-ordination platform to accomplish this. The Swedish Agency for Economic and Regional Development is its secretariat.

The forum is divided into two groups: one that promotes dialogue between national- and regional-level politicians, and one that fosters dialogue among national- and regional-level civil servants. There are about 50 regular participants at the political level, who convene 4 times a year. Additional participants, such as ministers, state secretaries and directors within state agencies, can be invited on an ad hoc basis, depending on the agenda topics. The civil servant meeting, which brings together regional-level civil servants at the director level, occurs three times a year.

Having two levels of conversation means that the right people are at each table. The political forum ensures that the highest-level decision makers are engaged on high-level regional development issues, making these issues visible on the political level and favouring political buy-in. Discussion on the civil servant level brings the right people to the table for the strategy's implementation.

Sources: OECD (2017[39]), *OECD Territorial Reviews: Sweden 2017: Monitoring Progress in Multi-level Governance and Rural Policy*, https://doi.org/10.1787/9789264268883-en; OECD (2020[6]), *The Future of Regional Development and Public Investment in Wales, United Kingdom*, https://doi.org/10.1787/e6f5201d-en.

Political support and financial incentives are missing to favour cross-government co-ordination and collaboration for regional development

This section explores two missing puzzle pieces for cross-government working to advance regional development in Estonia: political support and financial incentives. National civil servants recognise that these two forces would help to encourage ministries to work together for regional development, but both are hard to come by. Political support is difficult to secure due to political turnover and shifting priorities, and civil servants often lack channels to elevate regional concerns to high-level decision makers. Financial incentives to work together on regional development are currently largely limited to one region. The section ends with recommendations for putting these two puzzle pieces in place by embedding regional priorities in high-level political discussions, providing more direct financial incentives to work together on regional development and making indirect financial incentives more explicit.

In Estonia, political buy-in is considered a precondition for sustained cross-government co-ordination and collaboration for regional development, but it is hard to secure and maintain (OECD, 2025[38]). Political turnover and shifting political priorities compound the difficulty of sustaining long-term, cross-ministerial co-ordination and collaboration. At the same time, civil servants who want to co-ordinate more meaningfully across ministries sometimes struggle to be heard by the political level: they may lack the channels, motivation or time to elevate their discussions to high-level decision makers within their respective ministries (OECD, 2024[16]; 2025[38]). Without political awareness and buy-in, efforts to enhance cross-government co-operation for regional development stand little chance of becoming high-priority or institutionalised. The Economic Cabinet presents a good example of how political awareness and buy-in results in a formal co-ordination platform at the highest level (its focus on high-profile economic questions, such as how to improve Estonia's competitiveness, and on rising security concerns certainly helps to raise political awareness and buy-in).

Another missing piece of the puzzle is a financial incentive for ministries to take a co-ordinated regional approach. Estonia's experience with regional policies shows that financial incentives work to encourage ministries to take this kind of approach. The Estonian Government funds a handful of regional programmes (Estonian Ministry of Regional Affairs and Agriculture, 2023[3]). One of its regional programmes is dedicated to Ida-Viru county in Northeast Estonia, a region bordering Russia that has experienced a dwindling oil shale industry (Invest in Estonia, n.d.[40]; Estonian Ministry of Finance, 2023[41]). The region is the focus of the Ida-Viru County Action Plan, an initiative involving multiple ministries that outlines the central government's activities targeted at the development of the area (Estonian Ministry of Regional Affairs and Agriculture, 2023[42]). It receives funding through regionally specific national budget contributions and EU Just Transition Funds to support initiatives in the region[8] (Estonian Ministry of Regional Affairs and Agriculture, 2025[43]). Funding for this region provides an incentive for ministries to adopt a regional lens for Ida-Viru county (OECD, 2024[44]) A variety of ministries have already introduced and participated in interventions tailored to the region. For example, the Ministry of Economic Affairs and Communication issued a regulation that provides financial support for Ida-Viru business investment to diversify the economy, promote renewable energy and create new jobs (Eurofound, 2022[45]; Estonian Ministry of Economic Affairs and Communications, 2024[46]). In addition, the Ministry of Social Affairs created a fund for laid-off shale oil workers (Just Transition, 2021[47]). The example of Northeast Estonia shows that financial incentives help to encourage ministries to co-operate with their peers on planning and implementing regional development.

Filling these two gaps means raising the prominence of regional development at the political level and expanding financial incentives to work together:

- To raise the political prominence of regional development, a recommendation from the previous section is also relevant here: the Ministry of Regional Affairs and Agriculture could work to integrate a regional perspective into the workings of the Economic Cabinet. This approach makes sense not only because the cabinet is a cross-government body with significant influence over regional economic development but also because it would increase the political visibility of regional issues by ensuring they are regularly discussed at the highest levels of government.
- To create financial incentives to work together for regional development, the ministry could identify opportunities to link sectoral activities to funding opportunities through subnational development strategies, as Italy has done through its National Strategy for Inner Areas (Box 2.5). For example,

the Ministry of Regional Affairs and Agriculture could allocate some of its own funds to support initiatives under the pilot regional development agreements (Chapter 3). This initial funding could encourage other ministries to contribute if they recognise that it is also in their sector's interest (as in Iceland, Box 3.3). For example, the Ministries of Climate, of Transport Administration and of Regional Affairs and Agriculture all have an interest in optimising regional transport. Sharing the cost – including with other stakeholders like local authorities – of regional transport improvements foreseen in regional development plans can help them all meet their own objectives. EU funds can also serve as a powerful incentive for pooling sectoral investments into more regional projects, as shown in the above example of Just Transition Funds in Ida-Viru; several national and local government stakeholders mentioned the possibility of regionalising some EU funds to encourage co-ordinated national government action for regional development (ERR, 2025[48]).

Box 2.5. Creating a financial incentive to work together to implement Italy's National Strategy for Inner Areas

Italy's National Strategy for Inner Areas is an integrated strategy tailored to reduce demographic decline and land abandonment in many rural areas by improving the quality of essential services – education, health and mobility – and promoting opportunities for economic activity and jobs. The funding for the implementation of the strategy comes from multiple sources. It draws from EU funds (the European Regional Development Fund, the European Social Fund and the European Agricultural Fund for Rural Development) as well as national resources.

The governance of the strategy ensures that the way the strategy is executed – including how it is funded – requires cross-government collaboration. The national government created an inter-ministerial committee to align objectives, adapt sectoral policies to specific territorial needs and match different sources of financing. In addition, it set up a technical committee to select inner areas to be funded under the strategy. This technical committee consists of representatives from the Ministries of Education, of Health and of Agriculture, the Department for Cohesion Policy and subnational levels of government. The technical committee first assessed the various proposals of inner area projects submitted by regions, based on a framework with specific indicators to evaluate candidate area specificities (e.g. an area's distance to infrastructure and services, demographic trends, local authority capacity to implement projects, etc.). Second, the committee and other relevant experts conducted field missions to candidate areas to discuss development challenges and opportunities and specific project proposals with territorial actors. Following these two phases, the Technical Committee issued an investigation report for each area and a framework programme agreement was established for each project area as an implementation tool for inter-institutional co-operation. It lists all interventions to be conducted, the financial resources covering them, their schedule and related expected results.

Sources: Rossitti, M. et al. (2021[49]), "The Italian National Strategy for Inner Areas (SNAI): A critical analysis of the indicator grid", https://doi.org/10.3390/su13126927; Agenzia per la Coesione Territoriale (2022[50]), *National Strategy for Inner Areas*, https://www.agenziacoesione.gov.it/strategia-nazionale-aree-interne/?lang=en; OECD (2017[39]), *OECD Territorial Reviews: Sweden 2017: Monitoring Progress in Multi-level Governance and Rural Policy*, https://doi.org/10.1787/9789264268883-en; OECD (2020[6]), *The Future of Regional Development and Public Investment in Wales, United Kingdom*, https://doi.org/10.1787/e6f5201d-en; European Network for Rural Development (n.d.[51]), Strategy for Inner Areas, Italy, https://ec.europa.eu/enrd/sites/enrd/files/tg_smart-villages_case-study_it.pdf.

Summary of recommendations

To create structures and processes that favour cross-cutting and regionally focused policy, a prerequisite for a place-based approach, Estonia can:

1. **Strengthen the existing regional impact assessment mechanism**. The Estonian Government can increase accountability with a public "regional impact dashboard" on the Ministry of Regional Affairs and Agriculture website that displays anticipated regional impacts of new laws and strategies. Finally, it can provide guidance and training for staff conducting impact assessments in line ministries, including regional data, methodologies and good practices.
2. **Use regional development agreements to promote cross-government action**. Ministries can create a co-ordinated action plan outlining how they will work together to fulfil their commitments in pilot regional development agreements.
3. **Consider formalising cross-government co-ordination in new contracts**. Ministries can enter into contracts to make explicit how they will work together to realise Estonia 2035 objectives relevant to regional development.
4. **Create regular opportunities for ministries to come together and "connect the dots" for regional development, at the political and operational levels**. Regular, high-level dialogue among ministers about regional development – to take place, for example, during dedicated meetings of the new Economic Cabinet – can help ensure that regional development remains a strategic priority across government. Creating a regular opportunity for civil servants to come together on regional development issues through a steering committee for regional development can complement high-level dialogue. As an alternative, the government can strengthen the regional perspective in existing steering committees, for example by hosting a periodic discussion with the Ministry of Regional Affairs and Agriculture on the regional dimensions of the committee's work.

To set up the right incentives to motivate ministries to make policy in a cross-cutting and regionally focused way, Estonia can:

5. **Provide financial incentives to favour cross-government co-ordination and collaboration for regional development**. The Ministry of Regional Affairs and Agriculture could allocate initial funding to pilot regional development agreements, encouraging other ministries to co-invest in mutually beneficial initiatives within the agreements (e.g. regional transport improvements). This may involve regionalising some EU funds, replicating a positive effect in Ida-Viru where EU funds for the region encouraged ministries to co-operate with their peers on a regional plan and introduce their own initiatives to implement it.

Empowering subnational actors to enable a place-based approach

Strengthening subnational capacity and providing new opportunities to align planning among levels of government would further support a place-based approach in Estonia. Equipping municipalities with the strategic planning capacity, stakeholder engagement capacity and financial capacity to help them plan and invest for their region is an important step in this direction (although recommendations on local finances lie beyond the scope of this report). Meanwhile, county development plans could be used more effectively as a platform for fostering inter-municipal collaboration and aligning national and subnational priorities.

With continued focus on capacity building and partnership, local governments could play an increasingly active role in shaping the development of their regions.

This section is dedicated to how to empower subnational actors to enable a place-based approach. Empowering Estonian local authorities and other subnational actors (e.g. the pilot regional councils discussed in Chapter 3) requires that they have the capacity to plan and implement themselves, as well as the right levers to influence national decision making. This section considers these two facets. First, it explores how the Estonian Government can help local authorities overcome capacity challenges that limit the role of municipalities as strategy setters and implementers for regional development. Second, it considers how to strengthen vertical co-ordination between the national and local government levels to allow greater alignment between levels of government and greater bottom-up input for national sector policy. Ultimately, empowering subnational actors in these two ways will help both levels of government be better equipped to address regional needs and take advantage of regional opportunities.

Local capacity gaps limit the ability of local authorities to shape and drive regional development

To be able to drive regional development efforts, regions and their constituent municipalities need the capacity to contribute to the design and implementation of regional development initiatives. "Capacity" in this context encompasses the skills, structures, processes, time and resources necessary for municipalities to plan and implement. This sub-section analyses three areas in which local government capacity gaps limit the role of local authorities in shaping and driving regional development, namely spending and investment, strategic planning and stakeholder engagement. It includes recommendations to help the Estonian Government strengthen local capacity in these areas, including by strengthening guidance and skill building for strategic planning, and investing in competencies for stakeholder engagement among local authority staff.

There are limits to how much capacity building can achieve for small municipalities. Despite the 2017 Administrative-Territorial Reform, which reduced the number of municipalities and increased their average size (Box 2.6), many are too small to plan and implement effectively for regional development. During the reform, the Estonian Government used population size as a rough indicator of municipality capacity, establishing a threshold of 5 000 residents as a benchmark for a municipality's ability to function independently. The reform reduced but did not eliminate the number of municipalities falling below this threshold (15 remained) (Estonian Ministry of Finance, 2021[52]). Thus, based on national criteria, some municipalities remain that are too small to generate sufficient revenue to support the professional staff that would allow them to manage key functions effectively (Estonian Ministry of Finance, 2018[53]). This is where regional governance shows its value. Working at a regional scale, including through cross-jurisdiction co-operation as is the case with the pilot regional councils, can fill capacity gaps by providing expertise, administrative support and strategic co-ordination that smaller municipalities simply cannot develop or access on their own. Chapter 3, focused on pilot regional councils, picks up on this thread.

Box 2.6. Territorial administrative reforms in Estonia

In 2017, Estonia undertook a significant territorial-administrative- reform to enhance the capacity and efficiency of local governments. Prior to the reform, Estonia had 213 municipalities, many of which were small and lacked the resources to effectively provide public services. In 2016, the Administrative Reform Act stipulated that local government units must have more than 5 000 residents. The roll-out of this reform was initially conducted on a voluntary basis: the government promoted mergers for smaller local units, providing financial incentives to do so. After 2016, the government was empowered to take a more active role in organising mergers. The primary motivation was to strengthen local governance by creating larger, more capable municipalities that could ensure consistent regional development and improved service delivery.

Key changes include:

- Fewer and larger municipalities: The reform reduced the number of municipalities from 213 to 79, resulting in 15 urban and 64 rural municipalities. This consolidation was achieved through voluntary mergers, with some required by the state, to meet the criteria set forth in the Administrative Reform Act. The reform led to fewer and larger municipalities: the median population of municipalities increased nearly fourfold.
- No more county governments: The reform also affected Estonia's counties. County governments and governors were abolished as of 1 January 2018 and their responsibilities were transferred to relevant ministries and local governments. A new department in the Ministry of Finance – the Department of Regional Administration – adopted certain functions previously held by county governments (such as administering land privatisation processes, supervision over local vital statistics, electoral management and more). County development organisations, which take different legal forms (Chapter 3), maintain county planning functions. In addition to their use as planning regions, counties are also used as statistical regions for many government statistics.

Sources: CoR (n.d.[11]), *Division of Powers - Estonia*, European Committee of the Regions, https://portal.cor.europa.eu/divisionpowers/Pages/Estonia-Introduction.aspx;Kattai, K. et al. (2020[22]), "Analysis of Estonian regional development: Proposals for shaping regional governance models – Final report (Eesti regionaaltasandi arengu analüüs: Regionaalse valitsemise mudelite kujundamise ettepanekud – Lõpparuanne)", https://skytte.ut.ee/sites/default/files/2022-05/1.%20Regionaalne%20valitsemine%20lopparuanne_final.pdf; Noorkõiv, R. (2021[54]), "How Estonia's reforms empowered local government", https://decentralization.gov.ua/en/news/13820; OECD (n.d.[55]), *Country and Territory Profiles - Estonia*, https://www.sng-wofi.org/country-profiles/.

Limited local spending and investment capacity: Estonian local authorities have very little leeway to spend beyond executing their immediate competences

As decentralised government entities, Estonian local authorities play a significant role in managing public services and functions. Administrative decentralisation, i.e. redistributing tasks and functions from central to subnational governments, brings decision making closer to the people, allowing local governments to tailor services to the specific needs of their communities (OECD, 2019[56]). The European Committee of the Regions Decentralisation Index ranks Estonia second among EU Member States for administrative decentralisation (Denmark ranks first) (CoR, 2020[57]). In Estonia, local authorities manage a substantial number of responsibilities, some of which are shared with the national government (Table 2.3). Estonia's local government workforce comprised 52% of the total public sector in 2017, roughly in the middle of the distribution among OECD countries (OECD, 2019[58]). Maintaining an adequate local government workforce is critical to ensuring that municipalities can manage delegated responsibilities.

Table 2.3. Estonian local authorities manage a significant share of competences, many of which are shared with the national government

	Central government	Municipalities	Shared competence
General public services (administration)	Basic research activities	Issuance of building ordinances and permits	Administrative services (marriage, birth, etc.)
Public order, safety and defence	Police, firefighting, defence (military and civil)	Supervision of local regulations	Civil protection and emergency services, road traffic control (traffic signs and lights)
Economic affairs and transports	Construction and maintenance of national roads and railways; airports; support to enterprises; agriculture, rural development, irrigation; telecommunications; tourism, commerce, energy	Construction and maintenance of local roads and rails; special transport services (e.g. pupil and student transport)	Ports (waterways are financed by central government while local ports belong to municipalities); public transport administration; employment policies/services; manufacturing and construction; mining;
Environmental protection	Parks and green areas; soil and groundwater protection; climate protection	Waste management, sewerage, street cleaning	Nature preservation; noise and vibration abatement; air pollution; disaster management
Housing and community amenities	Electricity networks	Drinking water supply; public lighting; heating and amenities; cemeteries; housing and utilities (construction, renovation, management)	Spatial planning
Health	Pharmaceutical and medical products; general and specialised medical services; hospital services; preventative healthcare; public health services		Primary healthcare
Culture and recreation	Cultural heritage/monuments, national cultural facilities	Cultural facilities (local theatres, zoos, etc.); youth work; libraries; community centres; sports facilities	Museums
Education	Higher education; vocational education/training; special education; R&D	Maintenance of pre-school childcare institutions, primary schools	Secondary schools
Social welfare	Unemployment subsidies/benefits; immigration and integration of foreigners; support services for families	Provision of social services; social benefits grants and other social assistance; welfare services for the elderly; shelters and care homes; nurseries; social housing; child protection	Services for disabled persons

Source: OECD (2023[5]), "Questionnaire completed by the Estonian Ministry of Regional Affairs and Agriculture", OECD, Paris.

Despite their strong role in administration and service provision, local authorities have very little leeway to spend beyond their immediate competences. Subnational public spending is low in Estonia, only accounting for 9.6% of gross domestic product (GDP) and 24.3% of total public expenditure. This is significantly below OECD (16.6% and 39.5% respectively) and EU (17.1% and 34.4%) averages (OECD, 2024[59]). When combined with substantial delegated responsibilities, local authorities are left with little limited spending autonomy. With mandatory tasks taking up a large share of the budget – education alone accounts for more than a third of local budgets (OECD/UCLG, 2016[60]) – there is little room for discretionary spending.

In theory, local governments could increase their spending and investment capacity with greater own-source revenue, but this revenue has remained low and stagnant. Article 157 of the Estonian constitution grants local authorities the ability to manage their own budgets, levy and collect taxes, and impose duties (CoR, 2020[57]). The most significant source of own-source revenue comes from user charges and fees, and revenues from economic activities, a category that accounts for 8.7% of municipal revenues and can include, for example, school fees or property leasing (OECD/UCLG, 2022[61]). Municipal land tax has a small impact on municipal budget sheets, representing only 2.1% of total revenue in 2019 and only 0.22% of GDP (well below the OECD average of 1.0%) (OECD/UCLG, 2022[61]). This land tax, while not a significant source of revenue, is the largest local tax, accounting for 83.1% of municipal tax revenue in 2019. Municipalities set rates within central government limits (0.1-2.5% in 2021), though rates have remained largely unchanged since 2012 (averaging 2.4%). Other municipal taxes, including advertisement, road closure and parking charges, collectively made up just 1.1% of municipal tax revenue in 2020 (OECD/UCLG, 2022[61]). Overall, Estonia ranks at the bottom of all EU and OECD peers in terms of subnational own tax revenues (OECD, 2024[59]). In short, Estonian municipalities have a limited ability to generate their own revenues, leaving a core principle of decentralisation unmet: for decentralisation to function, decentralisation of spending responsibilities must be in tandem with increasing subnational capacity to generate own-source revenue (OECD, 2019[56]).

Low municipal own-source revenue as well as a tax reclassification have left Estonia's municipalities heavily reliant on national transfers. In 2022, Estonian subnational governments (municipalities) derived an average of 88.4% of their income from intergovernmental transfers and subsidies, compared to 44% across EU peers and 40% across OECD countries (OECD, 2024[59]). Estonia's revenue ratio (the share of subnational own-source revenues relative to total government revenues) is just 4%, one of the lowest in the European Union (CoR, 2020[57]). A 2014 change in the classification of taxes, which reclassified some national taxes shared with local authorities as grants rather than tax revenue, also contributed to the high proportion of national grants in local government revenue (OECD/UCLG, 2022[61]). The most significant of these taxes was personal income tax. It is important to note that the local government level has no discretion in setting rates for the personal income tax; the national government determines both the income tax rate and the municipal share of the revenue (OECD, 2022[62]). Ultimately, local authorities remain overwhelmingly dependent on the national government for their funding, with very limited ability to influence the amount of these transfers.

With most funding tied to earmarked grants, local authorities are effectively paid by the national government to deliver specific services that are national-level tasks (OECD, 2024[16]). Local governments not only depend on national transfers, but the bulk of these funds – 81% in 2021 – are earmarked for specific purposes by the national government (OECD, 2023[5]). Earmarked grants weaken flexibility in local decision making, which can have the perverse effect of penalising rather than rewarding efficiency. For example, a municipality that consolidates schools to cut costs cannot redirect the savings to other priorities; instead, it faces a cut in its grant in the subsequent budget period (OECD, 2022[62]). In recent years, small pots of money have been "unearmarked", notably funds for waste management and some social assistance (Congress of Local and Regional Authorities, 2023[63]), but the changes are marginal, leaving local authorities with little real autonomy to tailor spending of most national funds in a way that is responsive to local needs (OECD, 2024[16]).

Estonian local authorities do not have a sufficient revenue margin to invest in local and regional development, with some struggling to fund basic services (EC, 2024[64]). Estonian local governments spend less as a percentage of total public investment than their OECD and EU peers: in 2022, Estonian local governments contributed around 24% of total public expenditure compared to the nearly 40% contributed by subnational governments in OECD countries and about 34% in EU Member States (OECD, 2024[59]). Inflation has outpaced revenue increases in recent years, leaving local authorities in poor fiscal health (Minuomavalitsus, 2023[65]). Many struggle to deliver on their competences: data from 2019 show that many municipalities were struggling to meet basic service levels (as defined by the Estonian Government) in critical areas like crisis preparedness, child welfare and social welfare. For example, 58% were not meeting basic service expectations in providing social services for adults (Minuomavalitsus, 2020[66]).

Municipal finance reforms are beyond the scope of this report but Estonia can revisit previous recommendations for how to strengthen municipal finances. OECD reports have suggested that Estonia consider introducing a local income tax – for example, a surcharge "piggybacking" on top of the personal income tax levied by the central government – to provide municipalities with a stable, predictable revenue source (OECD, 2022[62]; 2011[67]). Other recommendations include adjusting the equalisation system and reducing earmarked grants (OECD, 2022[62]; 2011[67]). Estonia has made some progress towards providing municipalities with greater revenue in recent years. The 2017 Administrative-Territorial Reform came with measures to increase municipal revenues, including increasing the share of income tax going to local governments and the volume of the equalisation fund (ERR, 2019[68]; Estonian Ministry of Finance, 2022[69]). Additionally, in 2024, the government amended the Income Tax Act to gradually increase the share of pension income allocated to municipalities (Riigi Teataja, 2024[70]). The Ministry of Regional Affairs and Agriculture is also preparing a proposal to increase the revenue base of local governments, with a draft law expected in 2025 (Estonian Ministry of Regional Affairs and Agriculture, 2024[71]). For the moment, however, Estonia's fiscal decentralisation framework still largely leaves local governments dependent on the national level for their revenues and spending decisions.

Planning capacity: Estonia has low local and regional strategic planning capacity

Gaps in local and county planning could undermine Estonia's ability to make place-based policy. Municipalities are required to produce five-year development plans. They also participate in the development of county development strategies, which, in theory, align one municipality's planning with the planning of their neighbours. On paper, this system promises that municipalities co-operate to distil regional (county) priorities. These regional priorities could then create a common thread among municipalities to favour joint collaboration (and the efficiencies and new opportunities it could bring). In doing so, it could also attract entrepreneurs and investors whose needs align with a county's vision for local development. In practice, as discussed in this section, county development plans (Box 2.6) are not the drivers of local and regional development that they should be.

County development plans do not necessarily represent a strategic view of regional priorities. The guidelines for designing such plans suggest that each include a vision – a short statement of the future towards which the county is working (Estonian Ministry of Finance, 2018[72]). However, interviews with local authority staff suggest that the process of developing county development plans focuses more on reconciling diverse municipal interests than considering how to advance a collective vision (OECD, 2024[16]). In the planning process, there is no effective mechanism for local stakeholders to negotiate and identify collective interests around which to build the plans (Sootla and Kattai, 2018[10]; National Audit Office, 2017[73]). Instead, county development planning tends to aim for compromise among the priorities of all municipalities in each county to avoid hard trade-offs and political friction. Sometimes, according to focus group interviewees, county development plans were prepared not to guide action but to ensure eligibility for EU funding (OECD, 2024[16]). The result is a document that one local government staff member described as "a shopping list" (of local authority wishes), which does not necessarily reflect the collective development priorities or needs of the county (OECD, 2024[16]).

To help favour practical, strategic plans, the Ministry of Regional Affairs and Agriculture can consider updating its guidance for the preparation of county development plans. New guidance can encourage county development organisations to use a participatory process to create the collective vision, a step that is not currently addressed in detail in national government guidance. County development organisations can draw inspiration from the participatory foresight and vision-setting sessions that underpinned the development of pilot regional development agreements in Chapter 3. These sessions featured broad participation (involving a range of stakeholders beyond local governments themselves) and structured processes to explore potential futures and envision how to work together to bring about desired futures. Updated guidance can also introduce structured processes to help municipalities prioritise objectives collectively. It can, for example, introduce the range of decision support tools that counties can use to evaluate the regional impact of proposed objectives, from scenario planning to basic quantitative methods for impact analysis. To guard against a tendency to include objectives as a way to ensure eligibility for EU funding, updated guidance can urge the county development organisations to clearly distinguish between funded and unfunded initiatives when they draft the plans. Ultimately, these adjustments can help show local authorities a clear pathway to results, giving them a clear sense of how their decisions and actions will lead to change (Horlings, Roep and Wellbrock, 2018[74]).

Clarifying requirements and investing in skill building can also help favour high-quality county plans. The Ministry of Regional Affairs and Agriculture can also consider how to strengthen the skills of subnational actors to develop high-quality plans. The Estonian Government's action plan for local authority human resources development, which aims to ensure that local officials have the skills and knowledge necessary to achieve national and subnational strategic goals, is a good starting point. Indeed, a skills assessment featured in the action plan ranks development planning competences as one of its top priorities (Estonian Ministry of Regional Affairs and Agriculture, 2023[75]). Putting in place an online hub dedicated to resources on data-driven planning and prioritisation could help to build subnational strategic planning capacity. This could include – like in Czechia (Box 2.7) – links to sources of data for strategic planning, self-guided trainings, guidelines for good practices and examples of other county plans.

Box 2.7. A digital platform to support municipal planning in Czechia

The Ministry of Regional Development of Czechia created ObcePRO (https://www.obcepro.cz/), a web-based application to support municipalities in designing their municipal development strategies and programmes. The platform offers local governments practical planning tools such as statistical data, templates, samples of supporting documents and studies, e-learning courses, handbooks for municipalities, etc. Complete municipal development strategies are published on the webpage, so municipalities can learn from their peers. Since 2015, over 500 municipal development strategies (individual municipality or joint strategies) developed using the templates or guidance from the platform have been published on ObcePRO.

Sources: OECD (2023[76]), *OECD Public Governance Reviews: Czech Republic: Towards a More Modern and Effective Public Administration*, https://doi.org/10.1787/41fd9e5c-en; ENRD (n.d.[51]), "Strategy for Inner Areas - Italy", https://enrd.ec.europa.eu/sites/default/files/tg_smart-villages_case-study_it.pdf; Rossitti, M. et al. (2021[49]), "The Italian National Strategy for Inner Areas (SNAI): A critical analysis of the indicator grid", https://doi.org/10.3390/su13126927.

Engagement capacity: Local authorities could reinforce stakeholder engagement practices for regional development

Local authorities do not always exhibit strong and strategic engagement with local stakeholders, which limits their ability to understand and meet the needs of local businesses and residents. Some local stakeholders (entrepreneurs and representatives from other non-government organisations) believed that they were not engaged in a strategic way in the design and implementation of the local development plans (OECD, 2024[16]). One entrepreneur thought they were being asked to engage too much, at the expense of a more data-driven approach to decision making by the local authority ("Don't just ask entrepreneurs" was this entrepreneur's request) (OECD, 2024[16]). The need to strengthen data-driven and evidence-based decision making for development is also highlighted by local governments themselves[9] in a declaration on data-driven governance that underscores the importance of strengthening the competencies of local authority staff to make data-driven decisions (Rae Noortekonverents, 2023[77])). Building the ability of local authorities to engage meaningfully and strategically with stakeholders is critical to ensuring that local and regional development planning and initiatives reflect the actual needs and ambitions of residents and businesses.

With its emphasis on bottom-up input, a place-based approach relies on strong stakeholder engagement. Place-based policy should draw upon the perspectives of local actors – including the private sector and non-governmental organisations – to understand and address the challenges that communities face (OECD, 2025[2]). Placing stakeholder engagement at the centre of place-based policy development processes helps to ensure that policy is tailored to local conditions, contributing to the effectiveness of the policy. Strong stakeholder engagement can also help governments find unlikely allies. For example, in the Greater Copenhagen Region, Denmark, universities have acted as a neutral mediator between pharmaceutical companies and governments to foster industry growth (Beer, 2023[78]; Collinge and Gibney, 2010[79]). Realising the benefits of stakeholder engagement, however, requires meaningful and long-term strategic planning with stakeholders at the local level. Communities can best influence their own development when stakeholders actively participate in governing relevant initiatives, and where they are able to use their diverse knowledge sets to "collectively tackle complex policy problems" (Eversole, 2011[80]).

The national government can help build stakeholder engagement capacity by investing in the skills local authorities need to engage effectively with local actors. The examples shared above suggest that there may be capacity gaps – in skills, workforce or financial resources – that hinder stakeholder engagement at the local level. Increasing the human and financial resources of local authorities is beyond the scope of this paper. However, the national government can begin to address stakeholder engagement capacity gaps through skill building among local authority staff. To increase the ability of local authorities and county development organisations to develop meaningful and productive stakeholder engagement practices, the training hub for strategic planning (introduced above) can include a focus on stakeholder engagement. It can offer training or guidance materials on clarifying objectives for engagement, identifying and reaching stakeholders, manage stakeholder engagement processes and nurturing stakeholder relationships.

There are opportunities to further enhance strategic co-ordination among national and local governments

This section considers how national and local government planning and policy making for regional development can become more closely aligned. One of the factors that shapes vertical co-ordination – the lack of a regional level that can serve as an intermediary between national and local governments on regional development issues – is the focus of Chapter 3. This section focuses on another lever for vertical co-ordination: links between the strategies of the two tiers of government. Better alignment would allow both levels of government to find new opportunities for their activities to be more complementary and mutually reinforcing, and identify and manage trade-offs among the priorities of different levels (OECD, 2024[81]; 2014[82]). In addition to the recommendations to strengthen Estonia's use of regional councils (Chapter 3), this section presents one recommendation to help bridge the gap: making explicit the strategic planning links between government levels.

Estonia could enhance its strategic planning processes to find greater common ground between national and local priorities. Strategic planning for regional development is one potential mechanism to co-ordinate national and subnational interests and priorities (OECD, 2019[83]). According to the national planning law, a county plan's purpose is both to "express the interests of local governments and to balance national and local spatial development needs and interests" (Parliament of Estonia, 2015[84]). In Estonia, local and county development plans must be consistent with the relevant national strategic plans (Parliament of Estonia, 2015[84]; OECD, 2024[44]). However, subnational stakeholders suggested that national government could go further in consistently incorporating regional and local priorities into broader national strategies and policies (OECD, 2024[16]; ESPON, 2021[85]). Of course, with 79 local authorities, expecting ministries to fully accommodate every local nuance is unrealistic (Estonian Ministry of Regional Affairs and Agriculture, 2025[86]). Instead, the Estonian Government can focus on finding new areas of common ground between national and local plans and activities, to find new opportunities for mutually beneficial collaboration.

Finding new opportunities for common ground starts with clarifying links between the plans of the three different levels: national, county and local. The Estonian Government already maintains a national strategy platform that presents all of the government's strategic plans in one place (Estonian Government, 2021[87]). This platform could expand to include county development strategies, explaining how these and national strategies link, and where objectives at each level are complementary. Doing so can provide the national government with greater visibility on how its priorities complement subnational objectives. Estonia can draw inspiration from Czechia and Poland, which instituted strategic databases and integrated planning platforms that harmonised national and subnational priorities (Box 2.8).

Box 2.8. Tools to ensure strategic coherence across levels of government in Czechia and Poland

Czechia

The Ministry of Regional Development of Czechia has been tracking the compatibility of strategic goals at each level of government, including municipalities, through the Strategies Database. This database helps capture the linkages among already developed strategies. Building on this database, the OECD recommended that the Ministry of Regional Development further provide support to subnational governments in the early stages of planning to ensure the alignment of objectives and priorities. This could include, for example, training or workshops on how to "localise" regional/national policy objectives and frameworks, e.g. if a municipality aims to boost education, how can it design a strategy that addresses local needs while pursuing the national education policy objectives?

Poland

In 2020, the Polish parliament passed a number of amendments to the Act on Principles of Implementation of Development Policy. These include the introduction of the notion of a local development strategy (LDS) and the requirement that the spatial planning document and the socio-economic development diagnostic need to be included in the LDS to ensure stronger relations between the two policy documents, as in the past they were separated and not fully co-ordinated. The act also included a detailed process for elaborating a development strategy at the voivodeship, supra-local and municipal levels. A detailed process for consultation across levels of government for elaborating the LDS was also put in place. A municipal LDS needs to be submitted to the voivodeship board to ensure alignment with the voivodeship development and spatial policy and, in this case, with the supra-local development strategy.

Sources: OECD (2023[76]), *OECD Public Governance Reviews: Czech Republic: Towards a More Modern and Effective Public Administration*, https://doi.org/10.1787/41fd9e5c-en; OECD (2021[88]), *Better Governance, Planning and Services in Local Self-Governments in Poland*, https://doi.org/10.1787/550c3ff5-en.

Strategic alignment among levels of government can be reinforced through financial incentives set by the national government. In Estonia, the challenge is not only articulating broad developmental goals but agreeing on the tactical steps to achieve them (OECD, 2025[38]). Reserving resources for regional- or local-level projects that help advance national strategies can serve as an incentive for local authorities to align their initiatives with and actively contribute to the national agenda (the Korean New Deal featured in Box 2.9 provides an example). To do so, governments can make alignment with national priorities a condition of receiving funding, as demonstrated in the Swiss Federal Agglomeration Programmes (Box 2.9). Currently, Estonian municipalities can apply for EU funds under Cohesion Policy Objective 5

("Europe closer to citizens") to support collaborative projects under county development strategies, including for projects related to vocational training, supporting start-ups, research centres and rental housing stock. To support more integrated investment that advances national regional development objectives, Estonia could consider piloting a call under its EU Cohesion Policy national programme to select and support a set of complementary investment projects that also address cross-cutting regional development issues (e.g. the creation of specialised vocational training centres in renewable energy, with support for clean technology start-ups and research centres in a region, coupled with affordable housing schemes to provide students and new workers with housing). This approach – not currently in use in Estonia – gives concrete incentives for local authorities to be creative and develop projects that meet the needs at the local level and also advance national priorities. If the pilot call succeeds, this collaborative approach could contribute to advancing regional-level strategic planning and implementation (see Chapter 3).

Box 2.9. National-local co-financing as a way to ensure strategic alignment among levels of government

Encouraging local authorities to align with national policy through Korea's New Deal

In July 2020, Korea adopted the New Deal, aiming to accelerate remote work and education, promote low carbon and eco-friendly manufacturing, and lead the transformation into a green and digital economy. The deal planned to invest KRW 75.3 trillion in projects that are conducted outside of Greater Seoul. The majority of the spending is expected to be funded by the central government, covering KRW 42.6 trillion, or 57%, while local governments match those funds with a total of KRW 16.9 trillion. The balance is made up by private sector investments. The government assigned major projects, such as installing green technology in outdated government-leased apartments or artificial intelligence technology in traffic systems. Some of the planned projects are led by local governments, including the expansion of a robotics factory in Daegu and the establishment of an autonomous vehicle testing site in Sejong. The plan also creates special economic zones by providing fiscal and tax support while lifting regulations. In July 2021, the government announced an upgrade of the Korean New Deal: the Korean New Deal 2.0. Under the plan, the government strengthened the Local New Deal (part of the overall Korean New Deal 2.0) by providing fiscal and administrative support to accelerate a series of selected local government projects.

Competitive grant financing of urban infrastructure in Switzerland

Across Switzerland, agglomeration areas have seen increased development, driving up infrastructure and transport funding needs. Many agglomerations face growing demand to address congestion on local roads and to enhance recreational and green spaces. The Swiss Federal Agglomeration Programmes, funded and administered through the Federal Road and Agglomeration Traffic Fund, provide competitive grants for transport infrastructure in agglomerations. The federal fund contributes 30% to 50% of the funding necessary for selected investment projects, with higher quality projects able to receive a higher share of grants. Whether the projects help address local and regional traffic challenges is one of the evaluation criteria.

As a condition to access the grants, local authorities need to plan and implement projects in a co-ordinated way to address local needs. They need to harmonise their transportation, urban development and land-use plans and develop their agglomeration programmes jointly across administrative units. Some local authorities developed model projects precisely to generate collaboration and create an agglomeration programme to access the fund. Around 40 agglomerations throughout the country have participated in this programme. Many local authorities are currently developing the fourth generation of their programmes: one example is the programme for the Schaffhausen area, which focuses on promoting pedestrian and bicycle traffic and enhancing settlement street spaces.

Sources: OECD (2021[89]), *Korea - Korean New Deal*, https://infrastructure-toolkit.oecd.org/wp-content/uploads/Korea_NewDeal.pdf; Ministry of Economy and Finance of Korea (2021[90]), "Government announces Korean New Deal 2.0", https://english.moef.go.kr/pc/selectTbPressCenterDtl.do?boardCd=N0001&seq=5173; OECD (2022[91]), *G20-OECD Policy Toolkit to Mobilise Funding and Financing for Inclusive and Quality Infrastructure Investment in Regions and Cities*, https://doi.org/10.1787/99169ac9-en.

Summary of recommendations

To address a local spending and investment capacity gap and increase municipalities' own-source revenue so they can invest in local and regional development priorities, Estonia can:

1. **Revisit past recommendations on how to increase municipal fiscal autonomy**. While municipal finance reforms are beyond the scope of this report, Estonia could revisit past recommendations, including, for example, the introduction of a local income tax in the form of a surcharge "piggybacking" on top of the personal income tax levied by the central government, to reduce local government dependence on state revenues and increase their ability to fund regional and local development.

To address a local strategic planning capacity gap and increase the impact of subnational strategic plans, the country can:

2. **Update Estonian Government guidance for preparing county development plans to favour plans that are practical and strategic**. Updated guidance can encourage participatory vision setting, promote the use of decision support tools to assess regional impact and ensure a clear distinction between funded and unfunded initiatives.
3. **Invest in skill building in subnational civil servants developing county plans, through an online capacity-building hub**. An online hub dedicated to strategic planning skills for local government and county development organisations – developed under the leadership of the Ministry of Regional Affairs and Agriculture – can offer training, guidelines and good practice examples.

To strengthen local authority capacity to use stakeholder engagement to capture and act on local needs in local and regional development initiatives, Estonia can:

4. Use the capacity-building hub introduced above to share resources on stakeholder engagement for local civil servants and county development organisation staff. The hub can display resources focused on how local and regional civil servants can engage most effectively with local residents, companies and organisations (e.g. how to design and manage stakeholder engagement processes to benefit from stakeholder input and participation throughout planning and policy cycles).

To strengthen vertical co-ordination between national and local governments in order to favour complementary, mutually reinforcing regional development initiatives, Estonia can:

5. **Show the links between national strategies and subnational plans**. The national strategy platform can grow to feature county plans in addition to national plans, and identify and visualise the links and complementarities among plans at each level.
6. **Use financial incentives to encourage integrated local projects that advance national and subnational strategies**. This may include earmarking resources for region-specific projects within national strategies, or developing joint investment packages covering interlinked sectors and initiatives, to ensure that funding addresses local needs while supporting territorial development priorities.

Conclusion

This chapter presents how three factors limit Estonia's ability to take a fully place-based approach to regional development. First, the "one Estonia" approach taken by line ministries means that the national government does not routinely tailor its interventions to local and regional needs. Second, there are few opportunities for line ministries to come together and co-ordinate for regional development. Third, there is scope for the Estonian Government and local authorities to find new opportunities for mutually beneficial collaboration through strategic planning. At the same time, the capacity of local governments to plan for and act on their own needs and opportunities should be reinforced.

To address these three gaps, the Estonian Government can focus on building capacity and creating clear incentives for national and subnational actors to ensure that both are contributing optimally to regional development. For national ministries, this means ensuring that direct and indirect incentives favour taking a co-ordinated regional approach across the government, supported by strong co-ordination structures for regional development. On the subnational level, building capacity in spending and investment, strategic planning and engagement can help put local authorities in the driver's seat for regional development efforts. Finally, the Estonian Government can better leverage strategic planning as a way to identify new areas where national and local strategies align.

Estonia's pilot regional councils, discussed in the next chapter, can also play a role in overcoming these barriers. The pilot regional councils create a platform where national ministries, local governments and stakeholders collaborate on shared regional development priorities. They provide ministries with a focal point around which they can organise cross-sector collaboration for regional development. At the same time, they may build the capacity among local authorities to plan and implement for regional development. As Chapter 3 will explore, these regional councils represent a concrete step toward the place-based approach discussed in Chapter 1.

References

Agenzia per la Coesione Territoriale (2022), *National Strategy for Inner Areas*, https://www.agenziacoesione.gov.it/strategia-nazionale-aree-interne/?lang=en. [50]

Barca, F., P. McCann and A. Rodríguez-Pose (2012), "The case for regional development intervention: Place-based versus place-neutral approaches", *Journal of Regional Science*, Vol. 52/1, pp. 1-166, https://doi.org/10.1111/j.1467-9787.2011.00756.x. [96]

Beer, A. (2023), "The governance of place-based policies now and in the future?", OECD-EC High-Level Workshop Series: Place-Based Policies for the Future, OECD, Paris, https://www.oecd.org/content/dam/oecd/en/about/projects/cfe/place-based-policies-for-the-future/the-governance-of-place-based-policies-now-and-in-the-future.pdf. [78]

Braga de Macedo, J., J. Oliveira Martins and B. Rocha (2014), "Are complementary reforms a "luxury" for developing countries?", *Journal of Comparative Economics*, Vol. 42/2, pp. 417-435, https://doi.org/10.1016/j.jce.2013.06.003. [35]

Bryce, B. (2024), "Rural Proofing: Lessons from OECD countries and potential application to health", *OECD Regional Development Papers*, No. 73, OECD Publishing, Paris,, https://doi.org/10.1787/4011899a-en. [27]

Central Estonian Pilot Regional Council (2024), "Draft Regional Development Agreement". [37]

Collinge, C. and J. Gibney (2010), "Place-making and the limitations of spatial leadership: Reflections on the Øresund", *Policy Studies*, Vol. 31/4, pp. 475-489, https://doi.org/10.1080/01442871003723432. [79]

Congress of Local and Regional Authorities (2023), "Monitoring the implementation of the European Charter of Local Self-Government (Euroopa Kohalike Omavalitsuste Harta rakendamise seire)", https://www.agri.ee/sites/default/files/documents/2024-06/2023-FINAL-ET-Monitoring-European%20Charter-local-Self-government-Estonia.pdf. [63]

CoR (2020), *Decentralisation Index - Estonia*, European Committee of the Regions, https://portal.cor.europa.eu/divisionpowers/Pages/Decentralization-Index.aspx?countryName=estonia# (accessed on 6 January 2025). [57]

CoR (n.d.), *Division of Powers - Estonia*, European Committee of the Regions, https://portal.cor.europa.eu/divisionpowers/Pages/Estonia-Introduction.aspx (accessed on 12 February 2025). [11]

DAERA (2018), *A Guide to the Rural Needs Act (Northern Ireland) 2016 for Public Authorities (Revised)*, Department of Agriculture, Environment and Rural Affairs of Northern Ireland, https://www.daera-ni.gov.uk/publications/guide-rural-needs-act-northern-ireland-2016-public-authorities-revised (accessed on 14 March 2025). [26]

EC (2024), *2024 Country Report - Estonia: Recommendation for a Council Recommendation on the Economic, Social, Employment, Structural and Budgetary Policies of Estonia*, European Commission, https://economy-finance.ec.europa.eu/document/download/34698aa7-9514-41bc-9c64-e97fb70a741e_en?filename=SWD_2024_606_1_EN_Estonia.pdf. [64]

EC (2023), "EU Cohesion Policy: Just Transition Fund finances a new facility to produce rare earths magnets in Estonia", European Commission, https://ec.europa.eu/regional_policy/whats-new/newsroom/28-06-2023-eu-cohesion-policy-just-transition-fund-finances-a-new-facility-to-produce-rare-earths-magnets-in-estonia_en (accessed on 27 February 2025). [92]

ENRD (n.d.), "Strategy for Inner Areas - Italy", European Network for Rural Development, https://enrd.ec.europa.eu/sites/default/files/tg_smart-villages_case-study_it.pdf. [51]

ERR (2025), "Minister stands firm on regional representatives amid coalition pushback", https://news.err.ee/1609626290/minister-stands-firm-on-regional-representatives-amid-coalition-pushback. [48]

ERR (2024), "Läänemets valitsuse majanduskabinetist: turumajanduse aeg on läbi", https://www.err.ee/1609478114/laanemets-valitsuse-majanduskabinetist-turumajanduse-aeg-on-labi. [34]

ERR (2019), "Lääneranna municipality wants to change the local government revenue system (Lääneranna vald tahab muuta omavalitsuste sissetulekute süsteemi)", https://www.err.ee/953241/laaneranna-vald-tahab-muuta-omavalitsuste-sissetulekute-susteemi. [68]

ESPON (2021), *Regional Strategies for Sustainable and Inclusive Territorial Development - Estonia*, https://archive.espon.eu/sites/default/files/attachments/Regional%20strategies%20for%20sustainable%20and%20inclusive%20territorial%20development%20-%20Estonia.pdf. [85]

Estonian Government (2023), *Estonia 2035: Action Plan of the Government of the Republic (11 May 2023)*, https://valitsus.ee/media/6506/download. [18]

Estonian Government (2021), *Current Development Plans (Kehtivad valdkonna arengukavad)*, https://www.valitsus.ee/strateegia-eesti-2035-arengukavad-ja-planeering/strateegilised-arengudokumendid/kehtivad (accessed on 25 February 2025). [87]

Estonian Government (2021), "Green policy steering committee discusses potential for hydrogen use in Estonia", https://www.valitsus.ee/en/news/green-policy-steering-committee-discusses-potential-hydrogen-use-estonia. [31]

Estonian Government (2021), *Regional Policy Program 2021-2024 [Regionaalpoliitika programm 2021-2024]*, https://www.fin.ee/media/2654/download (accessed on 7 January 2025). [4]

Estonian Government (1999), *Estonian Regional Development Strategy (Approved by the Government of the Republic of Estonia on November 16, 1999, Agenda Item No. 24)*, https://web.archive.org/web/20140513132451/http://www.siseministeerium.ee/failid/reg_strategia.rtf (accessed on 7 January 2025). [7]

Estonian Government (1994), *Regional policy concept*, https://www.riigiteataja.ee/akt/30494 (accessed on 7 January 2025). [12]

Estonian Ministry of Culture (2021), *Cultural Development Plan 2021-2030 (Kultuuri arengukava 2021-2030)*, https://www.kul.ee/kultuur2030. [32]

Estonian Ministry of Economic Affairs and Communications (2024), *Regulation: Support for Investments in Ida-Viru Business*, https://eas.ee/wp-content/uploads/2024/01/regulation_ida-viru_investments_grant.pdf. [46]

Estonian Ministry of Economic Affairs and Communications (2020), *Transport and Mobility Development Plan 2021-2035*, https://kliimaministeerium.ee/sites/default/files/documents/2023-09/Transpordi%20ja%20liikuvuse%20arengukava%202021-2035_EN%20%281%29.pdf (accessed on 21 February 2025). [17]

Estonian Ministry of Education and Research (2021), *Education Strategy 2021-2035*, https://www.hm.ee/sites/default/files/documents/2022-10/haridusvaldkonna_arengukava_2035_kinnitatud_vv_eng_0.pdf (accessed on 11 March 2025). [15]

Estonian Ministry of Finance (2023), "Võrklaev: EU support is of great importance for the development of Ida-Viru County", https://www.fin.ee/en/news/vorklaev-eu-support-great-importance-development-ida-viru-county. [41]

Estonian Ministry of Finance (2022), *Monitoring Report - Five Years of Administrative Reform (Seireraport "Viis aastat haldusreformist")*, https://www.fin.ee/sites/default/files/documents/2022-10/HR%20seireraport%202022_0.pdf. [69]

Estonian Ministry of Finance (2021), *Administrative-Territorial Reform*, https://www.fin.ee/en/administrative-territorial-reform. [52]

Estonian Ministry of Finance (2021), *Regional Development Action Plan (Regionaalse arengu tegevuskava)*, https://www.fin.ee/media/5696/download (accessed on 11 March 2025). [9]

Estonian Ministry of Finance (2019), *2018 Monitoring Report on the Implementation of the Estonian Regional Development Strategy 2014-2020 (Eesti regionaalarengu strateegia 2014-2020 elluviimise 2018. aasta seirearuanne)*. [23]

Estonian Ministry of Finance (2018), *Administrative Reform 2017: Collection of Articles – Decisions, Background, Implementation (Haldusreform 2017: Artiklikogumik – otsused, taustad, elluviimine)*, https://www.agri.ee/sites/default/files/documents/2023-06/v%C3%A4ljaanne-2018-haldusreform-2017-artiklikogumik.pdf (accessed on 21 February 2025). [53]

Estonian Ministry of Finance (2018), *County Development Strategy Guide (Maakonna arengustrateegia koostamise juhend)*, https://www.fin.ee/media/2460/download (accessed on 6 March 2025). [72]

Estonian Ministry of Justice and Digital Affairs (n.d.), *Impact Definition Checklist (Mõjude määratlemise kontrollküsimustik)*, https://www.justdigi.ee/oigusloome-arendamine/hea-oigusloome-ja-normitehnika/oigustloovate-aktide-mojude-hindamine. [20]

Estonian Ministry of Regional Affairs and Agriculture (2025), "Internal memorandum", Unpublished. [86]

Estonian Ministry of Regional Affairs and Agriculture (2025), *Regional subsidies (Regionaaltoetused)*, https://agri.ee/regionaalareng-uhistransport/regionaalareng-ja-poliitika/regionaaltoetused#2024. [43]

Estonian Ministry of Regional Affairs and Agriculture (2024), *Expanding the Revenue Base of Local Governments (Kohalike omavalitsuste tulubaasi võimaluste laiendamine)*, https://www.agri.ee/kohalike-omavalitsuste-tulubaasi-voimaluste-laiendamine (accessed on 21 January 2025). [71]

Estonian Ministry of Regional Affairs and Agriculture (2024), *Overview of the implementation of the regional development action plan in 2023 (Ülevaade regionaalse arengu tegevuskava elluviimisest 2023. aastal)*, https://www.agri.ee/sites/default/files/documents/2024-10/tegevuskava-retk-seire-%C3%BClevaade-2023.pdf. [30]

Estonian Ministry of Regional Affairs and Agriculture (2024), *Regional development action plan (Regionaalse arengu tegevuskava)*, https://agri.ee/sites/default/files/documents/2024-10/tegevuskava-retk-2024-09.pdf. [29]

Estonian Ministry of Regional Affairs and Agriculture (2023), *Action Plan for the Development of Local Government Human Resources 2022-2025: Foundations (Tegevuskava KOV inimvara arendamine 2022-2025: Lähtealused)*, https://www.agri.ee/sites/default/files/documents/2023-06/tegevuskava-kov-inimvara-arendamine-2022-2025-l%C3%A4htealused.pdf. [75]

Estonian Ministry of Regional Affairs and Agriculture (2023), *Ida-Viru County (Ida-Virumaa)*, https://www.agri.ee/regionaalareng-uhistransport/regionaalareng-ja-poliitika/ida-virumaa. [42]

Estonian Ministry of Regional Affairs and Agriculture (2023), *Regional Development and Policy*, https://www.agri.ee/en/regional-development-and-policy. [3]

Estonian Ministry of Regional Affairs and Agriculture (n.d.), *National Spatial Plan Estonia 2050*, https://www.riigiplaneering.ee/sites/default/files/documents/2024-02/YRP_kokkuv6te_eng_esitatud.pdf. [14]

Eurofound (2022), *Support for Investments in Ida-Viru Business to Move Away from Oil-shale Production*, https://static.eurofound.europa.eu/covid19db/cases/EE-2022-26_2913.html. [45]

Eversole, R. (2011), "Community agency and community engagement: Re-theorising participation in governance", *Journal of Public Policy*, Vol. 31/1, pp. 51-71, https://doi.org/10.1017/s0143814x10000206. [80]

Ferry, M. (2021), "Pulling things together: Regional policy coordination approaches and drivers in Europe", *Policy and Society*, Vol. 40/1, pp. 37-57, https://doi.org/10.1080/14494035.2021.1934985. [19]

Horlings, L., D. Roep and W. Wellbrock (2018), "The role of leadership in place-based development and building institutional arrangements", *Local Economy: The Journal of the Local Economy Policy Unit*, Vol. 33/3, pp. 245-268, https://doi.org/10.1177/0269094218763050. [74]

Invest in Estonia (n.d.), *East Estonia*, https://investinestonia.com/regions/east-estonia/ida-viru-county/. [40]

Invest in Southeast Estonia (n.d.), *Homepage*, https://southeastestonia.com/en/. [95]

Just Transition (2021), "Estonia: Fund covering loss of wages", https://www.just-transition.info/bestpractices/estonia-fund-covering-loss-of-wages/. [47]

Kattai, K. et al. (2020), "Analysis of Estonian regional development: Proposals for shaping regional governance models – Final report (Eesti regionaaltasandi arengu analüüs: Regionaalse valitsemise mudelite kujundamise ettepanekud – Lõpparuanne)", https://skytte.ut.ee/sites/default/files/2022-05/1.%20Regionaalne%20valitsemine%20lopparuanne_final.pdf. [22]

Loewen, B. (2018), "Towards territorial cohesion? Path dependence and path innovation of regional policy in Central and Eastern Europe", Dissertation, University of Tartu, https://www.researchgate.net/profile/Bradley-Loewen/publication/329895254_Towards_territorial_cohesion_Path_dependence_and_path_innovation_of_regional_policy_in_Central_and_Eastern_Europe/links/5c210e22299bf12be39820ab/Towards-territorial-cohesion-Path-de. [13]

Ministry of Economy and Finance of Korea (2021), "Government announces Korean New Deal 2.0", https://english.moef.go.kr/pc/selectTbPressCenterDtl.do?boardCd=N0001&seq=5173. [90]

Minuomavalitsus (2023), "Many local governments have had a difficult financial situation for a long time [Paljudel omavalitsustel on olnud pikemat aega keeruline finantsolukord]", https://minuomavalitsus.ee/uudised/paljudel-omavalitsustel-olnud-pikemat-aega-keeruline-finantsolukord (accessed on 9 January 2025). [65]

Minuomavalitsus (2020), "Service levels highlight both local government and national challenges [Teenustasemed toovad välja nii omavalitsuste kui ka üle-eestilised väljakutsed]", https://minuomavalitsus.ee/uudised/teenustasemed-toovad-valja-nii-omavalitsuste-kui-ka-ule-eestilised-valjakutsed (accessed on 9 January 2025). [66]

National Audit Office (2017), *Problems Related to the Use of European Union and Other Infrastructure Support in Local Governments*, https://www.riigikontroll.ee/tabid/206/Audit/2454/language/en-US/Default.aspx. [73]

Noorkõiv, R. (2021), "How Estonia's reforms empowered local government", Decentralization, https://decentralization.gov.ua/en/news/13820. [54]

OECD (2025), "OECD workshop with the Government of Estonia: Co-ordinating for impact: Supporting a regional approach across the Estonian government", Unpublished, OECD, Paris. [38]

OECD (2025), *Place-Based Policies for the Future*, OECD Publishing, Paris, https://doi.org/10.1787/e5ff6716-en. [2]

OECD (2024), "Focus group interviews conducted in May 2024", OECD, Paris. [16]

OECD (2024), *Regional Governance and Public Investment in Wales, United Kingdom: Moving Forward Together*, OECD Multi-level Governance Studies, OECD Publishing, Paris, https://doi.org/10.1787/e143e94d-en. [8]

OECD (2024), "Stakeholder interviews", Unpublished, OECD, Paris. [44]

OECD (2024), *Subnational Government Structure and Finance - 2024 Edition*, OECD, Paris, https://www.oecd.org/content/dam/oecd/en/topics/policy-issues/subnational-finance-and-investment/subnational-governments-infrastructure-finance-2024.pdf/_jcr_content/renditions/original./subnational-governments-infrastructure-finance-2024.pdf. [59]

OECD (2024), *Unleashing Policy Coherence to Achieve the SDGs: An Assessment of Governance Mechanisms*, OECD Publishing, Paris, https://doi.org/10.1787/a1c8dbf8-en. [81]

OECD (2023), *OECD Public Governance Reviews: Czech Republic: Towards a More Modern and Effective Public Administration*, OECD Public Governance Reviews, OECD Publishing, Paris, https://doi.org/10.1787/41fd9e5c-en. [76]

OECD (2023), "Questionnaire completed by the Estonian Ministry of Regional Affairs and Agriculture", OECD, Paris. [5]

OECD (2022), *G20-OECD Policy Toolkit to Mobilise Funding and Financing for Inclusive and Quality Infrastructure Investment in Regions and Cities*, OECD Publishing, Paris, https://doi.org/10.1787/99169ac9-en. [91]

OECD (2022), *Shrinking Smartly in Estonia: Preparing Regions for Demographic Change*, OECD Rural Studies, OECD Publishing, Paris, https://doi.org/10.1787/77cfe25e-en. [62]

OECD (2021), *Better Governance, Planning and Services in Local Self-Governments in Poland*, OECD Publishing, Paris, https://doi.org/10.1787/550c3ff5-en. [88]

OECD (2021), *Health at a Glance 2021: OECD Indicators*, OECD Publishing, Paris, https://doi.org/10.1787/ae3016b9-en. [24]

OECD (2021), *Korea - Korean New Deal*, OECD, Paris, https://infrastructure-toolkit.oecd.org/wp-content/uploads/Korea_NewDeal.pdf. [89]

OECD (2020), *Regional Policy for Greece Post-2020*, OECD Territorial Reviews, OECD Publishing, Paris, https://doi.org/10.1787/cedf09a5-en. [1]

OECD (2020), *Regulatory Impact Assessment*, OECD Best Practice Principles for Regulatory Policy, OECD Publishing, Paris, https://doi.org/10.1787/7a9638cb-en. [25]

OECD (2020), *The Future of Regional Development and Public Investment in Wales, United Kingdom*, OECD Multi-level Governance Studies, OECD Publishing, Paris, https://doi.org/10.1787/e6f5201d-en. [6]

OECD (2019), *Effective Multi-level Public Investment: OECD Principles in Action*, OECD Multi-level Governance Studies, OECD Publishing, Paris, https://doi.org/10.1787/c3bc625b-en. [83]

OECD (2019), *Government at a Glance 2019*, OECD Publishing, Paris, https://doi.org/10.1787/8ccf5c38-en. [58]

OECD (2019), *Making Decentralisation Work: A Handbook for Policy-Makers*, OECD Multi-level Governance Studies, OECD Publishing, Paris, https://doi.org/10.1787/g2g9faa7-en. [56]

OECD (2017), *OECD Territorial Reviews: Sweden 2017: Monitoring Progress in Multi-level Governance and Rural Policy*, OECD Territorial Reviews, OECD Publishing, Paris, https://doi.org/10.1787/9789264268883-en. [39]

OECD (2014), *Recommendation of the Council on Effective Public Investment Across Levels of Government*, OECD, Paris, https://legalinstruments.oecd.org/en/instruments/OECD-LEGAL-0402. [82]

OECD (2012), *Promoting Growth in All Regions*, OECD Regional Development Studies, OECD Publishing, Paris, https://doi.org/10.1787/9789264174634-en. [36]

OECD (2011), *Estonia: Towards a Single Government Approach*, OECD Public Governance Reviews, OECD Publishing, Paris, https://doi.org/10.1787/9789264104860-en. [67]

OECD (2011), *OECD Regional Outlook 2011: Building Resilient Regions for Stronger Economies*, OECD Publishing, Paris, https://doi.org/10.1787/9789264120983-en. [21]

OECD (n.d.), *Country and Territory Profiles - Estonia*, World Observatory on Subnational Government Finance and Investment, https://www.sng-wofi.org/country-profiles/. [55]

OECD/UCLG (2022), *Estonia Country Profile*, OECD/UCLG World Observatory on Subnational Government Finance and Investment, https://www.sng-wofi.org/country_profiles/estonia.html (accessed on 6 January 2025). [61]

OECD/UCLG (2016), *Estonia*, https://www.uclg-localfinance.org/sites/default/files/ESTONIA-EUROPE-V3.pdf. [60]

Parliament of Estonia (2015), *Planning Act*, https://www.riigiteataja.ee/en/eli/527062016001/consolide. [84]

Rae Noortekonverents (2023), "Data-driven management - The code to successful local government (Andmepõhine juhtimine - kood eduka kohaliku omavalitsuseni)", https://konverents.rae.ee/omavalitsuspaev/wp-content/uploads/sites/17/2023/09/OVP-Andmepohine-juhtimine-kood-eduka-omavalitsuseni-DEKLARATSIOON.pdf. [77]

Riigi Teataja (2024), *Income Tax Act Amendment Act (Tulumaksuseaduse muutmise seadus)*, https://www.riigiteataja.ee/akt/114082024001. [70]

Rossitti, M. et al. (2021), "The Italian National Strategy for Inner Areas (SNAI): A critical analysis of the indicator grid", *Sustainability*, Vol. 13/12, p. 6927, https://doi.org/10.3390/su13126927. [49]

SGI (2024), *Estonia - Coordination*, Sustainable Governance Indicators, https://www.sgi-network.org/2024/Estonia/Coordination. [33]

Shortall, S. and E. Sherry (2019), *Rural Proofing in Northern Ireland: An Overview and Recommendations on Guidance, Implementation and Governance*, https://www.afbini.gov.uk/publications/rural-proofing-northern-ireland-overview-and-recommendations. [28]

Sootla, G. and K. Kattai (2018), "Institutionalization of subnational governance in Estonia: European impacts and domestic adaptations", *Regional and Federal Studies*, Vol. 30/2, pp. 283-301, https://doi.org/10.1080/13597566.2018.1511979. [10]

Strauss, D. and J. Pickard (2024), "UK assessment of worker rights bill 'not fit for purpose', warns watchdog", Financial Times, https://www.ft.com/content/5360621f-dc54-41e1-82b9-43a157a2011f. [94]

Ühiskonnateaduste instituut (2023), "The end-of-year colloquium at Tallinn University summed up the year of local government cooperation and set goals for the future (Aastalõpu kollokvium Tallinna Ülikoolis võttis kokku omavalitsuste koostöö aasta ja seadis sihid edasiseks)", https://www.tlu.ee/yti/uudised/aastalopu-kollokvium-tallinna-ulikoolis-vottis-kokku-omavalitsuste-koostoo-aasta-ja (accessed on 28 February 2025). [93]

Notes

[1] I.e. designed and implemented without explicit consideration of geographical context or place-specific characteristics (Barca, McCann and Rodríguez-Pose, 2012[96]).

[2] Exceptions exist, such as the Science Programme, which involves both the Ministers of Education and Research and of Economic Affairs and Communications (OECD, 2024[16]).

[3] Not to be confused with South Estonia, this is a smaller area consisting of Võru, Valga and Põlva counties (Invest in Southeast Estonia, n.d.[95]).

[4] Measures for which county-level data are available.

[5] One example of governments imposing consequences for regulations that fail to meet impact assessment "screens" comes from the United Kingdom, where new regulatory proposals must undergo a Small and Micro Business Assessment (SaMBA) to evaluate their impact on small enterprises. Poor assessments can result in – and have resulted in – a negative evaluation by the country's Regulatory Policy Committee and requests to address specific issues (Strauss and Pickard, 2024[94]).

[6] The Ministries of Education and Research, of Justice, of the Environment, of Economic Affairs and Communications, of Finance, of Social Affairs, of Regional Affairs and Agriculture (previously the Ministry of Rural Affairs), of Foreign Affairs and the Government Office. In addition, it welcomes representatives from the Association of Estonian Cities and Municipalities and creative unions, as well as specialised experts (Estonian Ministry of Culture, 2021[32]).

[7] Even though the centre of government does not take a primary role in co-ordinating regional development, it is worth noting that experts have pointed to limited capacity on the part of the Government Office and prime minister to co-ordinate and monitor activities associated with Estonia 2035, and to undertake substantial evaluations of line ministry proposals for activities related to Estonia 2025 (OECD, 2011[67]; SGI, 2024[33]).

[8] Northeast Estonia is the only region that meets the criteria to receive EU Just Transition funds, which support territories most affected by the transition towards climate neutrality (EC, 2023[92]).

[9] Those participating in the 2023 Local Government Day, alongside the Association of Estonian Cities and Municipalities, national government representatives and others (Ühiskonnateaduste instituut, 2023[93]).

3 Experimenting with regional governance for a place-based approach to regional development

Estonia's experiment with pilot regional councils marks a step towards the more place-based approach to regional development discussed in Chapters 1 and 2. Introduced in Central and South Estonia, the pilot councils bring together representatives from national government, local governments and other regional stakeholders to chart a path forward for development in the two regions. This chapter presents the motivations to establish the councils, and distils lessons from the design, implementation and first results of the two pilots. It also explores how the Estonian Government can evaluate the experiment and consider potential pathways for scaling up regional governance.

Introduction

In 2023, the Estonian Government introduced two pilot regional councils to test a new approach to establishing and implementing regional development objectives. The government recognised that a new approach was needed to address what it called "a general dissatisfaction with the country's current limited regional perspective" (Estonian Ministry of Regional Affairs and Agriculture, 2025[1]). After exploring different options (Box 3.1), the government established two pilot regional councils – one in Central Estonia and one in South Estonia[1] – to create regional development agreements defining the development priorities and activities of the region. Bringing together national government, local government and other regional stakeholders, these councils also promised to serve as a "systematic two-way feedback loop" between plans and policy at the national and local levels.

Estonia's pilot regional councils represent a step towards laying the foundations for a place-based approach to regional development (Chapter 2), adapting the multi-level governance structure to favour cross-cutting responses to regional needs and opportunities. Place-based policy for regional development requires co-ordination and alignment across different policy areas and among levels of governments. Chapter 2 highlights that Estonia lacks both: i) co-ordination for regional development across different ministries on the national level; and ii) strong mechanisms to bridge national and local planning and policy making for regional development. The pilot regional councils help to address these two gaps by offering a structure to create common ground among national, regional and local actors. Ultimately, this approach promises to favour a co-ordinated regional approach among all of these actors to best address regional needs and take advantage of regional opportunities.

This chapter distils lessons from the experiment with regional councils. It traces the journey of the pilot councils through four phases: idea, implementation, results and future. It starts with the idea, exploring the Estonian Government's motivations for the councils. It then considers implementation, identifying lessons learnt from how the pilot councils were put into practice, including the need to broaden ministerial representation, clarify decision-making processes and harness stakeholder engagement. It continues with the results, assessing the agreements themselves to identify success factors, such as avoiding "shopping lists" of local demands, embedding enforcement mechanisms and building the capacity building of implementers. Finally, the chapter looks ahead to the future of the councils, exploring how the Estonian Government can evaluate and consider whether and how to scale up the pilots. In sum, this chapter can help the Estonian Government build on the experience of pilot councils to refine its approach, ensuring that future iterations live up to the promise of serving as a tool to advance place-based regional development.

Important note: **At time of writing, the draft agreements have been prepared but not yet signed.**

The chapter focuses on the text of the draft agreements available in Autumn 2024, which may change before they become finalised. This chapter is also unable to comment with certainty about who will sign the agreements, although the draft agreements provide an indicative list of draft signatories.

Box 3.1. The birth of an idea: A recognition that regional governance could be a tool to promote balanced growth

In 2020, an influential paper written by Estonian academics and experts made the case for regional governance in Estonia. The authors made some of the same observations as Chapter 1: growth in Estonia is concentrated in Harju County while other areas struggle to attract investment and skilled labour. As discussed in Chapter 2, local governments tend to lack sufficient influence over national strategic development planning and policy and sufficient capacity to plan and implement for development, which has limited the ability of Estonia to respond to regional challenges and take advantage of regional opportunities for development. Their answer to these issues was regional governance, and the authors proposed a range of alternative governance arrangements that would facilitate better co-ordination among national ministries, regional actors and local authorities.

Governance models proposed by the academics involved lesser or greater degrees of decentralisation and regional autonomy. One option was to strengthen county-level co-operation, requiring local governments to co-operate more systematically through formalised agreements and consolidating the various regional development and regional service institutions under the county-level associations of local governments (co-operative bodies that bring together local governments to promote balanced and sustainable development (Riigi Teataja, 2002[2])). Another model suggested the creation of regional councils to facilitate co-operation among local governments, the national government and other stakeholders, helping to ensure that regional priorities would be considered in national policy making. A more ambitious alternative was the establishment of regional self-governments, granting certain regions greater fiscal and legislative autonomy to tailor development policies to their specific needs. The authors also put forward a hybrid model, incorporating elements of both regional councils and co-ordination mechanisms, to balance local input with national oversight. The paper did not recommend a specific model above all others, but did propose a pilot project to begin testing a model (in addition to stakeholder engagement and political discussions).

Table 3.1. Advantages and risks of proposed governance models

Proposal	Advantages	Risks
Enhanced co-operation among local governments at the county level	Uses existing structures; low implementation cost	Limited authority and risk that regional decisions would be subordinated to local ones; harder to include national representatives
Creation of regional development councils	Improves co-ordination and allows for a greater range of representatives	Requires strong political support from national and local governments
Establishment of regional self-governments	Positive effects for democracy and subsidiarity; possibility of an independent and stable revenue base associated with its direct mandate; clear accountability	Potential for weakening local governments by removing tasks and associated funding; complex and costly; politically sensitive

Source: Kattai et al. (2020[3]), *Analysis of Estonian Regional Development: Proposals for Shaping Regional Governance Models – Final Report (Eesti regionaaltasandi arengu analüüs: Regionaalse valitsemise mudelite kujundamise ettepanekud – Lõpparuanne)*, https://skytte.ut.ee/sites/default/files/2022-05/1.%20Regionaalne%20valitsemine%20lopparuanne_final.pdf.

The idea: Three drivers behind the pilot regional councils

A trio of motivations drove the Estonian Government to pilot the councils: i) strengthening engagement between levels of government; ii) helping local governments achieve economies of scale by working regionally; and iii) tapping into the perspectives and resources of businesses and research institutions for regional development (Figure 3.1). First, the pilot regional councils were envisioned as a platform to strengthen engagement between local and national governments, a step towards more alignment between local-level planning and national-level policy and activities. Second, they aimed to help municipalities plan and work together more effectively on a larger scale. Finally, the councils sought to bring other stakeholders to the table, with the initial idea of deepening co-operation among government, businesses and researchers to harness their expertise and resources to drive regional development. This section explores these three drivers in detail, examining how each shaped the design of the pilot councils and how they were intended to address Estonia's regional development challenges.

Figure 3.1. A trio of motivations for establishing the regional councils

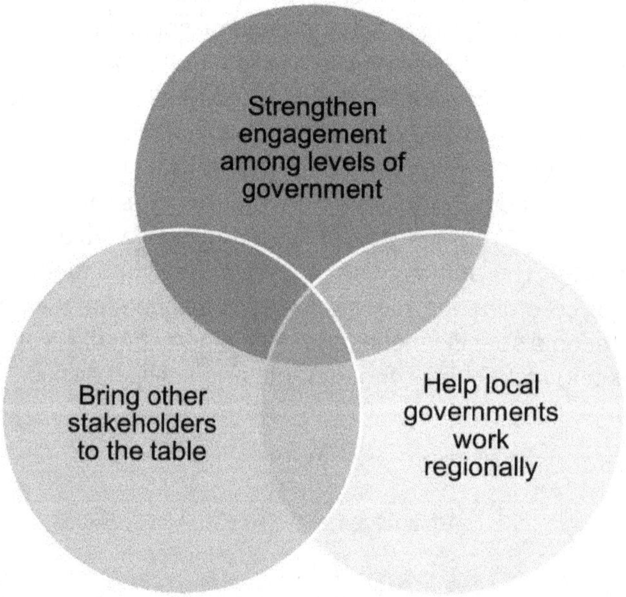

The councils were intended to support collaborative planning and collaboration among municipalities

In general, Estonian local authorities are small and shrinking in terms of their populations, which can limit their ability to attain economies of scale for service delivery and investment. Municipal mergers in 2017 decreased the number of municipalities from 213 to 79, but local governments remain small in terms of population size. Following the mergers, the average municipal population is 16 653, which puts it well below the average of OECD countries (40 107 inhabitants). Estonia's municipalities are small even when compared with its small nation peers: the average of other small unitary OECD and European Union (EU) countries is 30 804 inhabitants. In addition, Estonian municipalities are getting smaller: nearly 60% of its municipalities are shrinking (OECD, 2022[4]). Small municipalities can struggle to deliver public services and invest in the development due to their limited size and resources. As discussed in Chapter 2, the 2017 Administrative-Territorial Reform reduced but did not eliminate the number of municipalities deemed too small to function independently. For small municipalities, co-operation with their neighbours can be a way to deliver public services more efficiently and to invest at the right scale (Allain-Dupré, 2018[5]).

The pilot regional councils were intended to encourage Estonia's local governments to plan together, which can help them find opportunities to work together on a larger scale. One justification for putting in place regional governance structures is achieving economies of scale (along with a host of other justifications, such as achieving strategic co-ordination, gaining stronger administrative resources and capacities, and internalising cross-jurisdictional externalities). Regional co-operation can provide economies of scale[2] and lower transaction costs by encouraging subnational governments to operate on a larger scale (OECD, 2020[6]). Co-operative regions – the category of regional governance that best describes the pilot councils (Table 3.2) – can favour efficiencies by creating a structure within which municipalities collaborate rather than work in isolation (OECD, 2022[4]). The process the pilot regional councils were to undertake – which involved identifying shared regional priorities and aligning municipal strategies to create a regional development plan – promised to help municipalities find new areas for co-operation. Finding new areas for co-operation at the regional level would mean dealing with heterogeneity within regions (including, for example, an urban-rural mix in South Estonia as shown in Table 1.1) to find a common strategic direction. However, the Estonian Government did not designate specific areas for co-operation beyond planning. This meant that any opportunities to achieve greater scale for activities would need to be identified through the planning process itself.

Table 3.2. A range of regional governance models in OECD countries

Regional governance model	Description	Examples
Regions with legislative power	These regions have a high level of political autonomy, with their own constitutions, parliaments and governments. Responsibilities are large and defined by the constitution or similar documents. They have primary or secondary legislative powers and are characterised by their elected executive and deliberative bodies.	Federated states in federal countries (e.g. German *Länder*); autonomous communities in Spain
Decentralised regional governments	Self-governing legal entities with elected bodies in unitary or quasi-federal countries. They have some autonomy over their spending decisions, access to various sources of funding (grants, tax revenues, user charges) and may also borrow. They have elected deliberative and executive bodies but do not possess legislative powers.	Regions in France and Italy
Co-operative regions	Formed through the co-operation of existing local authorities to manage tasks that benefit from regional-level management, such as regional development, spatial planning and EU funds management. They generally have their own budget (funded by contributions from municipalities and central government transfers).	Associations of municipalities in Nordic countries; French intercommunal associations
Planning or statistical regions	Established by central governments for planning and statistical purposes. They have limited powers and primarily serve as platforms for discussion. In some cases, they have representative bodies and may manage EU funds. They often exist in countries with large municipalities or where regional governance is emerging.	NUTS 2 regions in the European Union; planning regions in Slovenia

Note: NUTS 2 regions are basic regions established within the EU's Nomenclature of Territorial Units for Statistics (NUTS) (Eurostat, n.d.[7]).
Source: OECD (2022[4])Regional Governance in OECD Countries: Trends, Typology and Tools, OECD Publishing, https://doi.org/10.1787/4d7c6483-en.

Co-operative regions, like the pilot regions, can help build economies of scale, not just in planning but in service delivery and administration. In general, this type of region forms through a collaboration among existing local governments to manage functions that benefit from co-ordination at a higher, regional level. The potential for economies of scale depends on the function in question, but common responsibilities include regional development, spatial planning and the management of public investment funds, including EU funding. Sometimes they have functions in public service provision. For example, Iceland's regional associations of municipalities are charged not only with preparing and implementing regional development plans for their regions, but also tasks delegated by municipalities like waste collection and the administration of school offices (OECD, 2022[8]). The scope of the work of co-operative regions usually reflects areas where regional-level operations add the greatest value (OECD, 2022[4]).

However, it would be a mistake to assume that the pilot regional councils alone would automatically translate to any greater co-ordination than joint planning. Shared regional plans can certainly support joint decision making and policy implementation among local authorities. At the very least, they create a shared vision of a development future to which constituent municipalities can align. Ideally, they detail actions that require municipal co-operation in order to implement. This is true in both regional development agreements, which unite local authorities to, for example, consolidate the organisation of public transport in South Estonia and create new vocational education opportunities in Central Estonia (Central Estonian Pilot Regional Council, 2024[9]; South Estonian Pilot Regional Council, 2024[10]). However, given that co-operation among municipalities is rare in Estonia, the country would need to address barriers that have historically limited co-operation to allow inter-municipal co-operation to flourish, including through regional councils and regional development agreements (Box 3.2).

Box 3.2. Inter-municipal co-operation in Estonia is rare, despite the benefits it could offer to small and shrinking municipalities

Inter-municipal co-operation offers a flexible and pragmatic tool for helping Estonia's municipalities improve service delivery, address the challenges of population decline and overcome capacity constraints. Inter-municipal co-operation could help Estonia's municipalities improve service efficiency and address challenges related to population decline. Economies of scale are particularly important for capital-intensive services such as education, infrastructure maintenance and waste management. By pooling resources, municipalities could provide higher-quality services at a lower cost. Additionally, inter-municipal co-operation can help maintain local democracy by enabling small municipalities to retain some decision-making power while benefitting from shared services.

Inter-municipal co-operation in Estonia remains limited despite the potential benefits it could offer. Following the 2017 Administrative-Territorial reform, some co-operative structures were maintained at the county level, particularly for public transport and spatial planning. However, compared to other OECD countries, Estonian municipalities have been slow to embrace inter-municipal co-operation. One key reason is that Estonian municipalities rely heavily on central government transfers, which weakens financial incentives for municipalities to collaborate voluntarily.

Focus group interviews suggested that, even when the will to collaborate is there, the practicalities often prevent civil servants from doing so. Local officials, already overburdened with their core tasks, often struggle to carve out the time and secure the necessary resources to engage in co-operation with other municipalities. For this reason, voluntary co-operation tends to occur only when an urgent need or a dedicated funding stream exists.

For inter-municipal co-operation to be more widely adopted in Estonia, the OECD has identified several barriers to be overcome. First, the legal framework for voluntary inter-municipal co-operation should be clarified to make agreements easier to establish and exit. Second, the transfer system could be adjusted to provide financial incentives for municipalities to co-operate. Third, national and countywide spatial plans should outline clearer guidelines for municipal collaboration in areas like education and infrastructure. Finally, the central government could play a more active role by supporting inter-municipal co-operation pilot projects, building local government administrative capacity and facilitating knowledge-sharing among municipalities.

Sources: OECD (2022[4]), *Shrinking Smartly in Estonia: Preparing Regions for Demographic Change*, https://doi.org/10.1787/77cfe25e-en; OECD (2024[11]), "Stakeholder interviews", OECD, Paris.

The pilot regional councils also promised to create a stronger connection among levels of government on regional development issues

County governments once served as a link between national and local government interests related to regional development, although they faced criticism for over-representing national needs. When county governments were still in place, state-appointed county governors were charged with ensuring the development of the county. Their county administrations developed county plans in co-operation with the national and municipal levels of government, including, for example, through negotiations with both national and local governments. They thus played a role in searching for common ground in the interests expressed by different stakeholders, ensuring that the county development plans included the different inputs in a complementary way. That is not to say that the county administrations performed this role as well as local actors would have liked; in fact, county plans at the time were subject to the criticism that national government needs were too prominent and also that these plans were not attached to state budget lines (Arenguseire Keskus, 2017[12]; OECD, 2011[13]). With the dissolution of county governments in 2018,[3] local authorities lost this process of negotiation between national and local interests. One group of experts went so far as to say: “with the abolition of county governments, the previous coherence between the central government and local governments at the county level disappeared” (Kattai et al., 2020, p. 16[3]).

Their replacements – the county development organisations – do not fill the same role of co-ordinator and mediator between levels of government. The legal forms of county development organisations vary: they may be municipal associations, county development agencies or simply a local government itself (Kattai et al., 2020[3]) – but they look very different from the previous county governments. Importantly, they lack the built-in national perspective that a state-appointed county governor provided. Thus, while there is a requirement for county plans to reflect national objectives (see Chapter 2), there is no longer a built-in mechanism that brings national and local governments together to consider how they can find common ground on and then advance the development of the territory.

The Estonian Government hoped the pilot regional councils would bring back one of the advantages of the county governments: strengthening the connection between levels of government on regional development issues. The pilot councils would serve as a mechanism to bring together national and local governments in a deliberative discussion, where each brings their own perspective, and seek to find areas of mutual benefit to carry forward together. This, in theory, could have two effects. First, bringing representatives from different sectors of the national government around the table to develop county plans could favour national support and guards against local government “shopping lists” (a complaint about today’s county plans, discussed further in Chapter 2). Second, it would elevate local voices to national-level decision making and encourage ministries to consider regional perspectives in policy making, something that is currently not routinely done. With national government council members coming from different ministries, the way national government is represented on the councils was also meant to advance greater cross-sector co-ordination (Chapter 2) (Estonian Government, 2023[14]).

Ultimately, the improved connection between levels of government offered by the pilot regional councils was meant to help both levels of government better address regional development issues. Even simple dialogue and information sharing with subnational governments can help national governments ensure that national policy and investment can better meet local needs, as discussed in the previous chapter (OECD, 2019[15]). The councils’ negotiation process also promised to encourage central and subnational levels of government align their objectives and activities, which also would help them avoid conflicting activities or misallocated resources. As the following sections will show, however, the way the regional councils and their agreements are designed and executed will determine whether they deliver fully on the benefits of better engagement between the two levels of government.

The councils were designed to bring other stakeholders to the table

One of the motivations behind the pilot regional councils was to foster collaboration among government, businesses and research institutions, with a view towards harnessing their perspectives and resources to promote specialisation and competitiveness. The pilot regional councils aimed to integrate the voices of companies and research institutions into regional planning and set the stage for co-operation among all participating actors towards the agreements' objectives. Doing so, the Estonian Government believed, would offer two benefits:

- **Promote innovation in the two regions**: The Estonian Government's initial focus on bringing private and knowledge actors to the table was born of an early focus on innovation-led regional growth. At the beginning, the government envisioned a focus on research and development (R&D) and innovation as a way to promote regional competitiveness. To best identify and then act on opportunities for regional R&D and innovation, the initiators of the councils believed having the businesses and research institutions around the table was a must (Estonian Government, 2023[14]). This idea reflects the triple helix model of innovation, which emphasises close collaboration between among government, universities and the private sector. Collaboration among the three groups can create alignment between government priorities, academic research and private sector activity, so that, for example, the private sector is better able to turn scientific knowledge into commercial applications to drive economic growth (Etzkowitz, 2008[16]).
- **Ensure workforce needs for regional development goals are met**: The Estonian Government had asked pilot regional councils to define focus areas for regional development and wanted to ensure that there would be a workforce with the appropriate skills to take these areas forward (Estonian Government, 2023[14]). Thus, including educational institutions would encourage them to adjust their approach to prepare a workforce that could drive the regional development vision of the councils.

While the councils' focus quickly evolved to consider a broader range of regional development drivers, the core aim of bringing stakeholders to the table remained unchanged. The substantive focus of the pilot regional councils broadened from the initial focus on competitiveness and specialisation: the government and the council members recognised that the regions could benefit from considering a broader set of regional development drivers, including, for example, infrastructure and service delivery. Despite the shift in focus, the core principle of bringing stakeholders to the table remained, albeit with a different aim, no longer seeking opportunities for innovation but rather encouraging networked co-ordination to address complex regional development challenges.

The implementation: The pilot regional councils in practice

This section examines how the government's ambitions for the councils were translated into practice through the institutional design of the councils, and what design choices meant for the councils' ability to function effectively. It discusses three institutional design choices that shaped the pilots: who participated, how decisions were made and how stakeholders were engaged throughout the process. First, in terms of participation, while the councils successfully established a tripartite structure – including representatives from national government, local government and business and academia – narrow ministerial participation constrained their ability to influence national planning and policy. Next, the section explores decision making within the councils: during council negotiations, members struggled to balance their roles as independent advisors and representatives of their institutions, generating questions about on whose behalf they were participating: their institutions' or their own. Finally, the section looks at stakeholder engagement, which evolved over time to include a greater range of voices, granting the councils a broader perspective on regional needs and ambitions. The way each of these design choices played out in practice provides lessons on how to shape future councils.

Lesson 1: Broaden national engagement to support the agreements

The pilot regional councils were designed as a multi-level governance tool to unite national government, local government and stakeholders in driving the development of the two regions. Their tripartite structure reflects the Estonian Government's recognition that, while the government views addressing regional disparities as "primarily the responsibility of the central government", success depends on close collaboration with local governments and key stakeholders (Estonian Government, 2023[14]). Each group would play a different role:

- **National government**: The intention was that council members from the national government – nominated by relevant line ministries – would play a leading role in integrating regional needs into national policy frameworks and ensuring inter-ministerial co-operation to do so. They would ensure alignment between regional development agreements and national strategies, including sector strategies across government, adjusting their activities (including investment) where relevant to meet their commitments in the regional development agreements (Estonian Government, 2023[14]).
- **Local government**: The role of local government members was to reflect the priorities and needs of the municipalities in the region. Members, which may come from county development organisations or from larger local governments in the region (e.g. Tartu), are nominated by the development organisations of the counties in the region (Estonian Government, 2023[14]). In practice, representatives from local governments tended to be top leadership of county development organisations or elected officials (when it was established, the South Estonian Pilot Council included four mayors) (Estonian Ministry of Public Administration, 2023[17]).
- **Other key stakeholders**: This category includes other parties, such as regional businesses, universities and researchers, which should make up at least one-third of the council. As introduced above, the Estonian Government placed a strong focus on including members from businesses and universities in the pilots to favour regional development agreements that reflect the needs of local business and opportunities for regional innovation (Estonian Government, 2023[14]).

The pilot regional councils succeeded in gathering all three categories of participant, but national representation was limited. The government hoped that the pilot regional councils would unite a broad range of ministries with local governments, businesses and universities. Its concept note, sketching the contours of the councils, included a list of potential member organisations selected to ensure representation across the most critical issues of the councils' focus areas (originally regional specialisation and competitiveness, which evolved to consider regional development more broadly as described above). The Estonian Government confirmed the final composition of each council through a decree that named the individual members. While the final councils had roughly equal numbers from each of the three key participant categories, the group of national government representatives was narrower than outlined in the concept note (Table 3.3). Beyond the Ministries of Finance and of Agriculture,[4] both councils included representatives from only two additional ministries: the Ministry of Education and Research, and the Ministry of Economic Affairs and Communications (Estonian Ministry of Public Administration, 2023[17]; 2023[18]). One additional ministry participated in discussions, even though it was not a formal council member: the Ministry of Climate. This highlights the difficulty of securing engagement from line ministries in regional development, a challenge explored in detail in Chapter 2.

Table 3.3. Planned and actual members of the pilot regional councils

Issue area	Planned members	Actual members
County development planning	County development organisations and larger local government units (e.g. the city of Tartu)	Leadership of county development organisations and elected officials of local authorities
Entrepreneurship and innovation	Ministry of Economic Affairs and Communications; *Enterprise Estonia*	Ministry of Economic Affairs and Communications
Labour market	*Ministry of Social Affairs*; *Unemployment Insurance Fund*	
Education	Ministry of Education and Research; universities (including regional colleges); *vocational training institutions; state secondary schools*	Ministry of Education and Research; University of Tartu; University of Tartu Pärnu College
Blue economy and bioresources	Ministry of Agriculture (later, the Ministry of Regional Affairs and Agriculture)	Ministry of Agriculture (later, the Ministry of Regional Affairs and Agriculture)
Creative industries	*Ministry of Culture*	
Spatial planning	Ministry of Finance	Ministry of Finance (council members moved to the Ministry of Regional Affairs and Agriculture, where they continued serving as representatives)
Tourism	Ministry of Economic Affairs and Communications; *Enterprise Estonia*; *Destination Management Organisations*	Ministry of Economic Affairs and Communications
Research and development	Ministry of Education and Research; universities	Ministry of Education and Research, University of Tartu, University of Tartu Pärnu College
Entrepreneurship and business	Entrepreneurs and business organisations in the focal sectors	A wide range of entrepreneurs; Estonian Chamber of Commerce and Industry Tartu Office; Central Estonian Business Incubator
Other	For example, relevant non-profit organisations; foundations; *LEADER action groups*; *Ministry of the Interior*	Foundation Tartu 2024; experts

Note: Those categories of participant that were not represented on the councils are listed in italics.
LEADER action groups are groups of people and local organisations that form within the European LEADER programme, designed to involve local actors in rural areas in the development of their regions (European Leader Association for Rural Development, 2025[19]).
Source: Estonian Government (2023[14]), *Pilot Project on Regional Development Plans and Councils*.

For future regional councils, the Estonian Government can take steps to broaden ministerial representation. It can target ministries whose involvement would have strengthened past councils, such as those responsible for environment, finance and social affairs. As the pilot regional councils begin to show the results of their work, more ministries may naturally wish to be represented on the councils. To encourage wider participation, the Ministry of Regional Affairs and Agriculture can proactively communicate the results of the experiment to target line ministries. Its pitch can highlight how adopting a regional lens can help these ministries advance their sectoral objectives more effectively (discussed in Chapter 2). As shown in the example from Iceland (Box 3.3), the councils can also show their value as a ready-made “bridge” for engagement between national and local governments. Additionally, securing leadership-level attention for the councils, e.g. by ensuring regional council representation at the Economic Cabinet (discussed in Chapter 2), could help to attract stronger high-level commitment that would encourage line ministries to actively participate in regional development efforts.

Box 3.3. Regional Plans of Action show their value as a tool for engagement with municipalities in Iceland

Iceland's Regional Plans of Action are five-year agreements developed for each of the country's eight statistical regions. Introduced in 2012, they are the primary legal tool through which municipalities co-operate regionally and co-ordinate development priorities. The plans guide investments in priority areas related to regional development, cultural initiatives, and social progress. These include projects designed to strengthen local communities, support economic diversification, and enhance quality of life across Iceland's regions.

Ministries contribute funding to the implementation of the Regional Plans of Action, and the plans have become a mechanism for connecting national policy goals with local action. The Regional Plans of Actions started with two participating ministries, the Ministry of Infrastructure and the Ministry of Culture, Innovation and Higher Education, both of which contribute funding for the implementation of the plans. As time went on, the Ministry of the Environment, Energy and Climate decided to participate too, recognising the value of Regional Plans of Action as a bridge between national and local governments and a way to meet national objectives at the regional level. There is an expectation that the Ministry of Industries will take on a direct role in the agreements in the near future.

Over time, the plans have strengthened the regions' ability to develop and implement a shared strategic vision. At the end of the first five-year period, for example, an independent report on the results of the action plans reported that "the regional associations are now well equipped to take on increased responsibility and manage additional funding."

Sources: Iceland Ministry of Infrastructure (2023[20]), "Interview with the OECD", OECD, Paris; Icelandic Government Steering Group on Regional Affairs (2020[21]), *Sóknaráætlanir landshluta*, https://www.stjornarradid.is/verkefni/fleiri-rit/rit/2020/11/23/Greinargerd-um-soknaraaetlanir-landshluta-2015-2019/.

Lesson 2: Clarify council member roles to avoid an uneasy relationship between "council members as expert advisors" and "council members as signatories"

During the negotiation of the regional development agreements, council members were expected to act as expert advisors. The government specified that council members should not be considered direct representatives of their organisations (Estonian Government, 2023[14]). They were asked to make decisions beyond the narrow interest of their own organisations, instead focusing on big-picture regional needs. This meant applying their own sector, business, organisational lens to the work of the council and, for non-ministry council members, thinking as residents or interested community members of the region. This approach was intended, in part, to prevent the need for participants to align positions with their home institutions before meetings, allowing for more dynamic discussions. The council members were asked to contribute their expertise, rather than their representative voice (Estonian Ministry of Regional Affairs and Agriculture, 2023[22]). The government also acknowledged that some key stakeholders (e.g. non-profit organisations, businesses and local authorities not directly represented on the councils) would not have a seat at the table and tasked council members with considering their perspectives as well. By asking the councils to speak for them too, they were meant to function as more than just the sum of their parts (Estonian Government, 2023[14]).

At the same time, there was always an expectation that signatories would make concrete commitments for activities that would bring about agreed-upon regional development goals. While a group of expert advisors might be expected to conclude with a set of recommendations, the councils were asked to conclude with an agreement (Estonian Government, 2023[14]). The regional development agreements were envisioned as contracts, which requires that signatories commit to a set of mutual obligations (OECD, 2007[23]). The below excerpt from the minutes of one of the pilot regional councils shows how council members were asked to consider themselves both expert advisors and institutional representatives.

> "[The chair of the council] notes that one of the questions that arises is who this council is and who the council members represent, what is the substantive and legal competence of the council.
>
> [The Ministry of Finance council support member] suggested that in this case **the council members should be treated primarily as a body of experts** with a broader perspective, whose task in preparing a regional development agreement is not to represent the interests of just one organization, ministry or county. If the development agreement is ever signed, it is important **who exactly the signatories of the agreement represent** in doing so."
>
> *Excerpt from the minutes of the South Estonian Pilot Regional Council (Estonian Ministry of Regional Affairs and Agriculture, 2023[22])*

The unclear distinction between personal input and institutional representation created challenges for participants in decision making. Local government representatives sometimes hesitated to make decisions in meetings, uncertain whether they were expected to speak independently or as formal representatives of their organisations. Meeting minutes, for example, show council members reiterating that they lack a mandate to formally agree by signing onto – or commit funding to – the councils' goals (Estonian Ministry of Regional Affairs and Agriculture, 2024[24]; 2023[22]). Similarly, national government representatives often sought prior confirmation from their ministries before committing to decisions. This may be partly due to the level of officials sitting on the councils; they may not have felt sufficiently empowered to make commitments on behalf of their institutions. Whatever the root cause, questions about decision making and accountability reduced the ability of council members to make decisions and to commit to the resulting agreement.

For future regional councils, the Ministry of Regional Affairs and Agriculture could begin by establishing guidance on the role of council members. These guidelines should specify expectations around council members' formally representing their organisations (discussed in greater depth in the following paragraphs). These guidelines should also include information on decision making. For example, they can stipulate how council members will report back to their home institution, and when and how council members will have the option of validating their positions with their home institutions. These guidelines should be sent to potential council members with a request to share them with other decision makers in their organisation. The goal is to ensure that council members and their home institutions are aware of the expectations for council members so that neither the council member nor their colleagues balk at these demands during the process of developing the agreement.

If the government wants council members to serve both as expert advisors and as institutional signatories, it can clearly separate these functions within the agreement process. To sharpen the line between the two roles of council members – expert advisor and representative signatory – one option is to structure the agreement process in two distinct phases, making a clear distinction between consultation and negotiation (Box 3.4). Participants in each phase can have a different, clearly defined role:

1. **Problem and solution scoping phase**: During this stage, council members would act as independent experts, focusing on identifying regional challenges and opportunities beyond their own organisational interests. This phase would correspond to the consultation phase in Box 3.4.
2. **Agreement negotiation phase**: During this stage, council members would cease to serve as advisors, and instead step into their representative role to negotiate a final agreement among signatories. This phase would be dedicated to arriving at a final agreement that aligns with the institutional priorities of signatories, one they are comfortable signing. Participation in this phase

may differ slightly from the previous phase. First, some council members may not plan on signing the agreements (this holds true even for the current pilots: the list of expected signatories on the two draft agreements, for example, does not include any of the entrepreneurs who participated) (Central and South Estonian Pilot Regional Councils, 2024[25]). At the same time, some other bodies may wish to sign the agreement, even if they did not participate as council members (for example, local authorities without direct representation on the councils or other relevant ministries).

During this stage, signatories are acting as representatives of their organisations, with the goal of negotiating strong and formal organisational commitments in the final agreement. To make sure that signatories are speaking with the voice of their organisations, councils could work into the schedule opportunities for signatories to consult with their home institutions in advance of key decisions. There is precedent for this already: the South Estonian Pilot Council solicited written responses by council members to documents produced by a working group, including official response letters with ministers' signatures (Estonian Ministry of Regional Affairs and Agriculture, 2024[26]).

Box 3.4. The stages of the contractual process

Contracts among levels of government typically follow a multi-stage process to arrive at an agreement, consisting of:

1. **Consultation**: This initial phase involves identifying shared priorities, assessing regional needs and engaging a broad range of stakeholders, from public authorities to civil society. This phase may be lengthy and involved: for example, in France, a two-year consultation process leading to State-Region Contracts brought together national and regional actors to define investment priorities collaboratively. Designing shared objectives is facilitated by the use of indicators agreed upon by all so priorities are clearly evidence-based.
2. **Negotiation and signature**: In this stage, formal agreements are drafted and negotiated between legitimate representatives of central and subnational governments. This stage sees parties defining the roles, responsibilities and funding mechanisms that will shape the activities under the contract. In order to not forget any key stakeholder and formalise the system for negotiation, it is useful to produce an "institutional mapping" clarifying "who does what and with whom." During the negotiation of the French State-Region Contracts, parties pay special consideration to sequencing and financial contributions (which may, although not systematically, include transfers from the national government).
3. **Implementation**: This phase translates commitments into action. Depending on the contents of the agreement, it may involve not only the contracting governments but also private actors, associations and other local institutions.
4. **Enforcement**: Contracts should have mechanisms in place to ensure that both parties meet their obligations and to resolve conflicts if they arise, as described in greater depth in the section. For example, Italy's Pacts for the South between Italian regions or cities and the national government included provisions for regular six-month reviews and allow for sanctions if milestones are not met.
5. **Evaluation**: Ex post evaluation helps assess performance, learn from experience and adjust future contracts. Carefully defined indicators will help parties know whether the contract has met objectives, whether new funding is needed, whether it should be renewed and, if this features in the agreement, whether rewards or sanctions should be given to parties.

Sources: Charbit, C. and O. Romano (2017[27]), "Governing together: An international review of contracts across levels of government for regional development", https://doi.org/10.1787/ff7c8ac4-en; Charbit, C. (2025[28]), "Slides: State-Regions Contracts to support administrative reforms and regional development", OECD Webinar on State-Regions Contracts - 11 April 2025.

An alternative approach would be to separate advisory and signatory roles within the regional governance model. The councils could be split into a dual structure: one body focused on strategic guidance and expertise (including private sector, civil society and academia) and another tasked with decision making and implementation (comprising institutional signatories, such as municipalities or representatives nominated by municipalities and relevant national ministries). In this model, the central government could engage primarily with the signatory group through formal negotiations and oversight mechanisms, while the agreements still benefit from the contributions of the advisory group in shaping priorities and assessing progress.

Future regional councils could be encouraged to include relational aspects to their contracts (Box 3.5) when parties are able to agree to objectives but not yet define the steps and actions necessary to reach them. For example, take the proposed objective in the draft South Estonian Regional Development Agreement to ensure that the region's enterprises can access renewable energy at an economically favourable price (South Estonian Pilot Regional Council, 2024[29]): instead of defining the tasks that this objective would entail in a set of transactional commitments, the agreement could include a relational commitment that details how parties will work together to bring about the commitment. Signatories could agree to work together with local government to meet the shared objective of ensuring new businesses have access to the energy they need without excessive upfront costs, within a specified co-operation and decision-making structure. Doing so can still lay a strong foundation for implementation, with signatories committing to working together within a specified framework and towards a specified objective, while allowing the steps and activities to be defined as they become clear.

Box 3.5. Transactional versus relational contracts

Experts make a distinction between transactional contracts, which rigidly define obligations in advance, and relational contracts, which establish a framework for ongoing co-operation.

- **Transactional contracts** resemble market exchanges, relying on formal rules and legal enforcement to manage well-defined tasks and contingencies. They are best suited for simple co-ordination problems, where all relevant outcomes and obligations can be anticipated.
- **Relational contracts** are designed for long-term co-operation under conditions of uncertainty. Rather than detailing fixed actions, these contracts establish governance frameworks that facilitate trust, learning and adaptive collaboration. They are especially effective where goals cannot be fully specified ex ante.

In practice, many contracts combine both: for example, agreements that require signatories to achieve specific targets may also include open-ended provisions that are defined during implementation.

Source: OECD (2007[23]), *Linking Regions and Central Governments: Contracts for Regional Development*, https://doi.org/10.1787/9789264008755-en.

Lesson 3: Design stakeholder engagement for well-rounded agreements

With a limited membership, future regional councils must look beyond their ranks to best represent regional interests in the agreements. Regional development involves complex, multi-dimensional issues, as described in Chapter 2. A relatively narrow representation of public sector, private sector and academic actors does not provide a comprehensive view of regional dynamics, needs and opportunities. Without broader engagement, the councils risk having blind spots in their final agreements. This is one reason why stakeholder engagement should play an important role in regional development agreement processes: it allows the councils to hear from a broader range of voices, including non-profit organisations and communities who have a direct stake in their region's development (OECD, 2023[30]). This engagement is crucial for gathering and co-producing the knowledge needed to identify regional needs and leverage regional assets (OECD, forthcoming[31]; 2018[32]).

Beyond informing decision making, stakeholder engagement can also play a role in maintaining the legitimacy of the pilot regional councils as well as future regional councils. The pilot councils are not elected bodies but rather appointed by the central government, although the government is supposed to take into account proposals from county development organisations and universities when appointing these members (Estonian Government, 2023[14]). Regional bodies without directly elected leaders can face criticism for lacking democratic legitimacy. Critics argue that the absence of direct elections can create a disconnect between regional governance bodies and citizens, as the leadership may not reflect the diverse interests and needs of the population they serve. Additionally, these bodies lack direct accountability to voters, who cannot remove representatives through elections (OECD, 2022[33]). Keeping stakeholders engaged helps to provide oversight and accountability, ensuring that councils act in the best interest of their regions.

To develop their agreements, the pilot regional councils drew on input from multiple stakeholder groups. At the outset, the planned stakeholder engagement prioritised businesses, with focus areas for development to be identified using regional data analysis and entrepreneur interviews (Estonian Government, 2023[14]). The Estonian Government recognised that relying solely on quantitative data and interviews with entrepreneurs would not provide a full picture of regional challenges and assets. It worked with the OECD to broaden input into the agreements by involving a wider range of stakeholders in foresight/futures and vision-setting workshops in each region. These workshops – designed to explore potential futures and begin to develop a shared vision for regional development in each region (described in Chapter 1) – brought together a diverse group of regional stakeholders. Participants included a range of local government officials, national government ministries, county development organisation representatives, tourism and cultural sector representatives, a representative from a local hospital, even a member of the Estonian parliament from one of the regions, as well as a range of business and industry representatives (OECD, 2023[34]). Broadening engagement through these workshops helped capture a fuller picture of regional strengths, challenges and aspirations.

Future regional councils should preserve an emphasis on broad engagement. They may consider starting with inclusive foresight/futures and vision-setting workshops that bring a wide range of stakeholders together to collectively define regional challenges, opportunities and aspirations. Starting with a collective exploration of the future of the regions gives regional councils something to aim towards, laying the foundation for an agreement that can best serve the regions. Following this broad visioning phase, councils can then narrow their engagement to target groups during the drafting phase, for example, entrepreneurs, industry groups and sector-specific experts. At this stage, the focus of the engagement shifts from developing a collective foundation for the regional development agreements to refining the "how", i.e. the activities needed to bring about the ambitions of the regions.

They should also make explicit how they will continue to engage with stakeholders during the implementation of the regional development agreements. Stakeholder engagement does not end with the signing of the agreements but will continue during implementation. Future regional councils should make explicit how they will keep stakeholders informed and/or involved during the implementation phase (while it is signatories that will implement the agreements – discussed in the following section – it is the councils who will monitor them). To keep up momentum, councils should establish regular engagement mechanisms and/or status updates with relevant parties, e.g. ministry officials, local authorities and advocacy groups, who play important roles in translating agreements into action. The Central Estonian Pilot Council has taken a first step in this direction by foreseeing in its agreement the organisation of regular conferences to share progress towards objectives (Central Estonian Pilot Regional Council, 2024[9]). These touchpoints can help to maintain support and commitment of relevant parties to the implementation of the agreements, which will be particularly important if changes arise during the implementation process that require additional funding, staff or time. It also requires the councils to be attuned to changes in priorities or leadership that could affect the ability of parties to implement the initiatives in the agreement (Michels and Wu, forthcoming[35]). Additionally, offering opportunities to scrutinise the decisions and outcomes of regional bodies through regular and transparent reporting can help mitigate the risk of decisions that counter the region's interests (OECD, 2022[33]).

Summary of recommendations

To broaden national government representation in the pilot regional councils, Estonia can:

1. **Share the pilot councils' results with target line ministries**, highlighting how engaging with the councils can advance participating ministries' goals. Cultivating greater political support for taking a regional approach – see recommendations in Chapter 2 – can encourage more ministries to seek representation on future regional councils.

To help overcome discomfort of regional council members to make decisions, Estonia can:

2. **Establish clear guidelines** on when members act as independent experts versus institutional representatives, potentially structuring the process into two phases, one for scoping and one for formal agreement negotiation that includes built-in opportunities for consultation with home institutions before decisions.
3. **Encourage councils to incorporate relational contract elements** into their agreements when they are able to agree to objectives, but not yet define the steps and actions to achieve them.

To ensure that stakeholder engagement captures a broad range of voices, both in shaping the agreement and throughout its implementation, Estonia can:

4. **Begin with inclusive foresight and vision-setting workshops**, bringing together diverse stakeholders to collectively define regional challenges and opportunities before narrowing engagement to targeted groups during the drafting phase.
5. **Establish clear mechanisms for ongoing engagement** during the implementation of the agreement to maintain support and resources, and adapt to changing needs.

The results: The two pilot regional development agreements

The work of the pilot regional councils led up to two draft regional development agreements. The previous sections explored the rationale behind the councils and how they functioned in practice. This section examines their first results: the pilot regional development agreements. It uses observations about the first pilot agreements to distil lessons on what future agreements should include to be credible, actionable and enforceable. In particular, it highlights three foundations for future agreements: securing credible commitments, clarifying implementation responsibilities and strengthening enforcement.

Lesson 4: For credible and actional agreements, continue to avoid "shopping lists" of unsupported commitments

Council members recognised that ministerial support was essential to realising the promises of the regional development agreements, both to favour a cross-government approach and to secure the resources needed for implementation. The Ministry of Regional Affairs and Agriculture's vision for the councils relied on broad ministerial participation, with line ministries expected to make concrete and co-ordinated commitments and provide resources to support implementation of the plans. Other council members from the two regions shared this perspective but were particularly focused on the funding and investment ministries could bring to their regions. They pointed to past experiences, such as the South Estonia Smart Specialisation Strategy, which struggled due to insufficient national backing (OECD, 2024[11]). To make the regional development agreements credible, the councils emphasised the need for each signatory to make clear and balanced commitments rather than producing documents that simply outlined local demands (OECD, 2024[36]). Without commitments from ministries across the national government, council members saw a risk that the agreements would be limited in their ability to promote a regionally co-ordinated approach.

Council members agreed that key to ministerial buy-in was avoiding "shopping lists" of local authority wishes for national government support, which the draft agreements have largely avoided. The fact that county plans sometimes included "shopping list" items – activities that local governments in the county would like the national government to support – is one of the reasons local and national government stakeholders consider them less effective than they could be (Chapter 2). Council members warned of the same thing happening with the regional development agreements (OECD, 2024[36]). As explored in Chapter 2, if an agreement is perceived as a collection of municipal funding requests without clear mutual benefits for national and local authorities, ministries may see little incentive to commit resources or policy support. The two pilot agreements have steered away from this and ministries evoked in the activities of the agreement are, for the most part, those who sat on the councils and helped shape the commitments. This should be maintained in future agreements.[5] Local authorities will still have the opportunity to voice their requests for their regions but during the negotiation of the agreement instead of at its release.

Future agreements should concentrate on ensuring "hard" commitments: direct and concrete commitments from signatories. These mutual commitments – a core feature of contracts among levels of government (Box 3.6) – provide the strongest foundation for implementation, ensuring ministries are aware of their commitments and can be held accountable to them. The councils can favour this kind of commitments from a wider group of ministries by broadening ministry representation on the councils (see recommendation on this in Chapter 2). However, signatories to the agreements do not necessarily have to be council members. Future regional councils can consider how to actively engage and negotiate with individual ministries outside the council to secure concrete commitments that align with their regional development objectives. Further, important non-council members could, for example, be integrated into collective negotiations during the negotiation phase of agreement preparation, as suggested above.

Box 3.6. Mutual, credible commitments are the backbone of agreements among levels of government

A contract represents a mutual agreement in which the parties commit themselves either to take specific actions, or to follow a jointly established decision-making process (depending on whether they are transactional or relational contracts, as explained in Box 3.5). Contracts define the mutual obligations of parties, including:

- **Authority**: who has the rights of decisions among parties.
- **Mutual duties**: the distribution of contributions, including funding, human capital, etc.
- **Enforcement**: mechanisms to enforce mutual contributions.

Clarifying responsibilities and making mutual commitments explicit makes contracts actionable and, combined with mechanisms for enforcement, make sure that signatories are held to their commitments.

Sources: (Charbit and Romano, 2017[27]) (OECD, 2007[23])

Lesson 5: Clarify who is doing what to implement the agreements and with what resources

The draft agreements do not always make clear who is doing what. Items in the draft agreements sometimes lack a responsible party (e.g. an activity dedicated to encouraging labour mobility in the Central Estonian agreement, which states simply "[t]he country should develop measures to encourage labour mobility" (Central and South Estonian Pilot Regional Councils, 2024[25]). Some tasks invoke multiple parties without specifying how the activity can be accomplished, like the task in the South Estonian agreement that states that "universities, companies and local governments [will strengthen] co-operation" (Central and South Estonian Pilot Regional Councils, 2024[25]). Without a specified lead, these tasks risk being neglected or poorly co-ordinated. It is important that all activities have a designated responsible party to ensure accountability and effective implementation.

The agreements also do not specify what resources will support implementation. The pilot councils received initial organisational support from the Estonian Government,[6] but they were not promised funding for implementation. Instead, they were to reach an agreement among signatories for how the implementation of their agreements would be funded. The agreements do not include a firm plan for implementation funding, although councils have ideas. The Central Estonian agreement includes two proposals for how to fund its implementation: either EUR 5 million per year from the national government, to which local governments would add EUR 1.5 million or a share of value added tax (VAT) (they provide 0.5% as an indicative figure) to fund implementation (Central and South Estonian Pilot Regional Councils, 2024[25]). These are just proposals, however, and there is no confirmed, long-term source of funding for implementing the agreements. Nor are there clear commitments from parties to fund specific initiatives. The most specific is a proposal in the Central Estonian agreement that says the Ministry of Regional Affairs and Agriculture should increase funding for the Central Estonia Scattered Settlement Program by 25%. Otherwise, activities in the agreements do not specify the resources that will be required, nor where they will come from. For example, a goal to develop a Central Estonian Science Park in the Central Estonian agreement only notes that the park will be founded by local governments, universities (Estonian University of Life Sciences) and the Ministry of Regional Affairs and Agriculture with no mention of who will contribute what resources towards this goal (Central Estonian Pilot Regional Council, 2024[9]). A lack of confirmed financial commitments from national and local governments, as well as other stakeholders, leaves the agreement at risk of stagnation.

Future regional councils can start with an institutional map that outlines the roles, responsibilities and linkages between all those involved in implementation, which can be formalised in a founding charter. This map should clearly identify which party is responsible for each task, including for tasks requiring collaboration across multiple entities, such as ministries, regional actors and local actors. By mapping these roles and relationships, the councils ensure that every party understands their responsibilities, and potential gaps in co-ordination can be more easily identified. In addition to showing roles, the maps should highlight the financial contributions from participants. This will help to reassure stakeholders that the agreements are feasible.

The agreement itself should also clearly define roles, responsibilities and resources. Doing so helps to ensure that agreements are realistic, avoiding, for example, unsupported tasks like the "shopping list" items for ministries discussed above. In addition, a well-structured contract creates effective enforcement mechanisms, discussed further below, to resolve conflicts and ensure commitments are upheld. Clarity on roles, responsibilities and resources makes it easier to hold parties accountable: it is simpler to measure contributions and overall progress during implementation when these factors are well-defined.

Lesson 6: Boost potential for success through strong enforcement mechanisms

While the pilot agreements include monitoring provisions, they lack built-in enforcement mechanisms to ensure that parties adhere to their commitments. The agreements do include provisions for monitoring. In Central Estonia, the agreement states that progress will be monitored by the pilot regional council annually, aided by the preparation of a monitoring report. The South Estonian agreement also includes a provision for annual monitoring and adds that the minister responsible for regional development will present an annual update to the Estonian Government. The Central Estonian agreement lacks explicitly defined performance indicators but mentions that they will be developed in the action plan, while the South Estonian agreement includes some broad performance indicators (e.g. regional gross domestic product growth and infrastructure targets). Neither, however, include any specific provisions for enforcement (Central and South Estonian Pilot Regional Councils, 2024[25]).

Without mechanisms to ensure that each party fulfils their commitments, the implementation of an agreement could flounder. One of the foundations of a contract is defining the binding reciprocal commitments of the parties, minimising ambiguities that could hinder implementation or create conflicts (Charbit, 2024[37]). Agreements can reduce the risk of non-co-operative behaviour through monitoring and evaluation systems that will allow stakeholders to know if parties are fulfilling their commitments (Charbit and Romano, 2017[27]). The pilot regional development agreements were right to include provisions for monitoring, even if they lack specific indicators. This monitoring is crucial to gauge whether contracts achieve their intended outcomes. It provides information that can help parties determine if a contract should be renewed, if additional resources are needed and if adjustments are required for future agreements. However, the agreements are missing monitoring's counterpart: enforcement. Contracts often include enforcement mechanisms such as penalties for non-compliance and provisions for third-party oversight, which ensure that commitments are met. Together, monitoring and enforcement help to ensure that the agreements are meeting signatories' objectives. Thus, the results of the monitoring exercise may show the councils where signatories are not delivering their contributions, but the councils will have no already-established mechanism to hold them to their commitments.

Like the pilot regional councils, future regional councils should include provisions for monitoring their agreements. Along with provisions for *how* monitoring should take place, agreements among levels of government should also include performance indicators. There is no one formula for determining the ideal performance indicators for an agreement but future councils can follow three rules of thumb. First, indicators should be measurable and linked to contract objectives. Second, the set of indicators should be broad enough in scope to mitigate the "streetlight effect", where parties focus on meeting their specific indicators rather than overall policy goals. Finally, they should be used in a way that promotes transparency and accountability, which can provide an incentive for good behaviour (Charbit and Romano, 2017[27]). The combination of these three principles can help create a system that helps parties track progress, identify obstacles early, keep agreements aligned with objectives and reinforce incentives for parties to follow through on their commitments.

Future regional councils should consider which enforcement mechanisms they can use to strengthen their agreements. Without provisions for enforcement, the agreements lack assurance that the commitments made by the different signatories are credible. Like monitoring and evaluation, enforcement can come from parties to the agreement (internal enforcement) or beyond the agreement (external enforcement):

- **Internal enforcement** can take the shape of reputational effects among agreement parties, which can create pressure for self-enforcement by these parties. Yardstick competition, where the relative performance of parties pushes other parties to behave efficiently, may also provide a source of internal enforcement. For agreements where money is on the line, financial awards can be adjusted based on performance.

To create opportunities for internal enforcement within the agreements, arrangements can be made for regular performance reports that present progress and measurable outcomes, creating pressure on parties to perform well. In addition, the agreements could tie agreed-upon financial disbursements to progress on specific targets (e.g. a specific project completed or a predefined number of businesses supported).

- **External enforcers** can include judges or independent agencies. The courts can serve the role of mediator, extracting information and using judicial procedures to solve conflicts. Independent agencies, international experts and media can use "revelation pressure", exerting pressure on parties by placing their actions or performance under scrutiny. Finally, stakeholders can also provide "social control", with stakeholders and citizens penalising parties for non-compliance, including at the ballot box.

  Future regional councils can put revelation pressure to work for them by creating regular opportunities for external scrutiny. For example, to create opportunities for external scrutiny of the agreements' implementation, agreements could specify that performance reports would be shared with specified external parties annually (e.g. through annual in-person reports to the Economic Cabinet, the Association of Estonian Cities and Municipalities and/or the network of county development organisations). Doing so would create an added layer of accountability, as these external actors would be able to scrutinise progress and highlight any shortcomings.

These mechanisms help to preserve motivation by creating incentives to deliver on commitments. Incentives can be positive, too: instead of only imposing penalties, agreements can specify rewards for positive contributions and results, for example, by maintaining a performance reserve of funds that are accessible if parties meet targets (Charbit and Romano, 2017[27]).

Summary of recommendations

To help ensure that future agreements are credible, actionable and realistic, Estonia can:

1. **Eliminate "shopping list" actions** for ministries in the agreements (unsupported requests that lack ministerial backing).
2. **Develop an institutional map** to clarify responsibilities, especially for multi-party initiatives and specify financial contributions. Ensure the agreements themselves also define roles, responsibilities and resources for implementation.

To hold signatories accountable to their commitments, Estonia can:

3. **Include provisions for monitoring the agreements**, including performance indicators that are measurable, linked to objectives, broad enough to encourage signatories to keep their eye on overall development objectives and used to enhance transparency and accountability.
4. **Specify enforcement mechanisms**, such as internal reputational incentives, financial performance-based adjustments or external oversight, in the agreements.

The future: Evaluating and learning from the experiment

The pilot regional councils have reached the right moment for an evaluation, and this section considers how the Estonian Government can evaluate the pilots. They have reached a natural inflection point, having largely completed their primary task of arriving at the regional development agreements (in itself a monumental task involving identifying regional strengths, challenges and ambitions before negotiating the text of the agreement). Evaluating the effectiveness of the pilot regional councils is essential before making decisions on their future: the Estonian Government will need to know if the experiments have yielded results that justify scaling them up and if any adjustments need to be made. This stocktake will help the Estonian Government understand which elements worked, which did not and what modifications may be required to ensure that any flaws in the first pilots are not replicated. This section draws upon core lessons for policy experiments from other OECD countries (Box 3.7) to consider how the Estonian Government should proceed as its pilot regional councils reach this stage.

Box 3.7. The ABCDs of policy experimentation for regional development

Policy experimentation refers to the structured testing of new approaches on a more limited scale – often through pilots – before wider implementation. Governments use policy experiments for all kinds of things: testing new service delivery models, piloting funding schemes, exploring alternative governance arrangements and more. They offer a lower-risk, evidence-informed way to introduce new initiatives, with the possibility of retiring them or refining them based on what actually works in context.

A review of OECD country experiences with policy experiments for regional development can provide some guidance for other countries designing experiments (or, in the case of a country like Estonia, implementing their experiment). These are the ABCDs of experimentation:

- **A – Articulate the scope**

  Experimenters should start by defining a clear rationale, goals and scope for the experiment, including the timeline, governance structure and evaluation checkpoints. While clarity upfront helps all participants know what to expect, allowing for flexibility in execution allows for real-time learning and adjustments during implementation (revisited in "C – Create learning cycles").
- **B – Bring stakeholders into the process**

  Participants in pilots are not passive subjects and experimenters can actively involve stakeholders, such as local governments, civil society and the private sector, in shaping, executing and evaluating the experiment.
- **C – Create learning cycles**

  A hallmark of an experimental approach is its ability to learn through action and reflection. Each experiment reaches a point when an evaluation is conducted: the "scale, shape or sunset" stage. This phase of the experiment involves a thorough review of outcomes. At this point, decision makers assess whether the experiment should be broadened ("scaled"), adjusted ("shaped") or retired ("sunset"). This stocktake is crucial for understanding which elements of the intervention worked, which did not and what modifications may be required. It may be at the "end" of an experiment, or at the intermediate stage between two stages of an experiment.
- **D – Dare to fall short**

  The inherent uncertainties and potential for visible failure may deter governments from taking an experimental approach. Countering this risk aversion requires that governments cultivate a safe environment for experimentation, including by shielding experiments with supportive legal frameworks and making clear that undesired results from an experiment will not result in cuts in resources. Governments can also take care to praise and share good experiments, not just good results, to help build a culture of experimentation. Finally, experimenters themselves should seek to recognise missteps and failures, and use them to learn.

Source: Durand, A. and M. Vincent (forthcoming[38]), "The ABCDs of policy experimentation", *OECD Working Paper*, OECD Publishing, Paris.

An evaluation starts by looking at an experiment's motivation and objectives. The Estonian Government can return to its original motivations for the experiment, which were described in the first section of this chapter: enabling economies of scale, fostering engagement among and across levels of government, and involving businesses and research institutions to promote regional competitiveness (as described earlier in the chapter, this has since broadened to involving a range of regional stakeholders for a more well-rounded approach to promoting regional development). It can also consider the government's objectives for the councils: what they were meant to do. The Estonian Government's concept note on the councils envisioned one overarching objective for the councils: to provide regional direction for activities and funding of national government (including the Ministry of Regional Affairs and Agriculture and line ministries) and local government, as well as funding from the European Union and other sources (e.g. the private sector) (Estonian Government, 2023[14]). Assessing these motivations and objectives against the actual outcomes of the experiment will help the Estonian Government determine whether and how well the councils have fulfilled their intended role.

The evaluation can then consider whether the experiment delivered on the ministry's hopes for it. None of the founding documents for the regional councils – the Estonian Government's original concept note, the establishing decrees – define how the pilot will be evaluated. The absence of predefined indicators and an evaluation framework makes ex post analysis of the councils challenging. Instead, the Ministry of Regional Affairs and Agriculture will have to define these retrospectively, developing indicators of pilot performance based on the ideas of what the pilots were supposed to do. By drawing a line from the intentions for the pilot regional councils to the actual results, the metrics that will help gauge whether the motivations and objectives behind the councils were satisfied (Table 3.4). Many of these indicators focus on process and immediate outputs of the pilots because the pilot regional councils are just now coming to an end of the drafting of their regional development agreements and these have not yet borne fruit that might be measurable in terms of broader outcomes (e.g. economic or well-being indicators). The ministry can also undertake a comparative analysis between pilot and non-pilot regions, where data are available.

These performance metrics do not have to be quantitative. Indeed, qualitative information plays an important role in evaluation when quantitative measures are not possible, and in order to contextualise quantitative measures (many of the metrics suggested in Table 3.4 are qualitative and rely on stakeholder perspectives, as discussed further below). For example, the Estonian Government may wish to gauge the impact of the pilots by understanding the extent to which the agreements fostered alignment in policy priorities among levels of government. To do so, it may be that the government could say that a certain number of sector plans included new references to agreed-upon regional priorities. It may also involve documenting how council discussions shaped funding decisions, influenced ministerial strategies or led to new mechanisms for alignment among levels of government. In those cases, the Estonian Government can describe the impact in a clear and objective way to allow other evaluators to assess at face value (OECD, 2008[39]). For the pilot regional councils, this can be as simple as including a qualitative description of these impacts (OECD, 2020[40]), explaining why the impact is relevant and the magnitude. While this type of evidence does not offer the rigour of a before-and-after or inter-regional quantitative comparison, it can still help the Ministry of Regional Affairs and Agriculture develop a well-rounded view of the performance and impact of the councils to make decisions about their future.

Table 3.4. Examples of qualitative and quantitative measures that could help evaluate the experiment of the pilot regional councils

Motivation/objective	Measures of success
Enabling economies of scale	• Increased investment or funding through co-ordination (e.g. additional funds invested in joint activities under the agreements) • Extent to which the agreements resulted in co-ordination among municipalities (e.g. from perception data via stakeholder interviews or surveys)
Fostering engagement across government levels	• Frequency of interactions between national and local governments through the councils or related activities (e.g. number of formal opportunities for national and local governments to come face-to-face to discuss regional development) • Extent to which the agreements fostered alignment in policy priorities among levels of government (e.g. from perception data via stakeholder interviews or surveys)
Involving businesses and research institutions to promote regional competitiveness	• Any concrete outcomes from new partnerships: new business activity, innovation projects, etc. (e.g. number of new innovation projects, or additional funds invested in innovation, springing from activities within the projects)
Providing regional direction for activities and funding	• Magnitude of funding commitments towards the councils' objectives from each source (e.g. funding from EU, national, local, private sector sources towards council objectives) • Impact on shaping funding decisions, co-ordination between different funding sources (e.g. from perception data via stakeholder interviews or surveys)

Soliciting stakeholder perspectives – and considering using an independent evaluator – can ensure that the evaluation benefits from broad and candid feedback. The pilot regional councils were designed to be collaborative, meaning that their effectiveness depends on the engagement and commitment of participants. For this reason, gathering information on the perspectives of participants, for example through a survey and interviews with council members, will be important to provide a fuller picture of the councils' impact. The Ministry of Regional Affairs and Agriculture can also collect the perspectives of stakeholders that did not sit on the councils but that do have a stake in their activities. These may include, for example, representatives from local authorities without direct representation on the councils, or ministries that had some degree of engagement with the councils even without serving as council members (e.g. the Ministry of Climate). Involving non-participants can provide additional insights into both the relevance and impact of the councils' work but also highlight any gaps in engagement and barriers to participation. The Ministry of Regional Affairs and Agriculture may choose to enlist the help of an evaluator external to the process to complete the evaluation. Making the evaluation independent can not only help to ensure that it is objective, but may also encourage participants to share more openly about their perspectives on the pilot regional councils.

If the Estonian Government decides to scale up the experiment, it should consider how to establish feedback loops to create new opportunities for learning and capacity building. Scaling up does not have to be an all-or-nothing decision. Rather than immediately scaling up the councils, Estonia could scale up in phases that allow for ongoing adjustments. If the Estonian Government decides it would like to bring additional powers (and resources, as discussed in the next paragraph) to the regional level, this sort of gradual "learning by monitoring" approach, such as that adopted by Sweden (Box 3.8), can also help the regions build capacity (OECD, 2018[32]). To this end, Estonia could take a phased approach to expanding the remit of the councils, where new responsibilities are introduced gradually and only after certain readiness thresholds are met. For instance, regions that meet certain conditions (e.g. demonstrating a strong process, e.g. sufficient stakeholder engagement, or certain desired results) could be the first to take on additional responsibility. By taking on new responsibility incrementally and meeting benchmarks, the regions would gradually increase their capacity, while the national government would gain greater confidence in their ability to manage expanded roles effectively.

Box 3.8. An iterative, experimental approach to regionalisation in Sweden

Sweden took a phased approach to regionalisation, refining its system through a series of pilot initiatives and evaluations. The process began in 1997 with the Regional Pilot Project, where certain regions were granted new competences, including responsibility for regional development planning, EU funding allocation and transport infrastructure. These pilot regions experimented with different governance structures, such as elected regional assemblies and indirectly elected councils.

A mid-term evaluation of the pilot regions led to the next phase: the introduction of Regional Development Councils in 2003 as a model available to all regions. These councils, formed through municipal co-operation, were given limited responsibilities compared to the pilot regions but still played a role in co-ordinating regional development initiatives.

Finally, in 2007, the Committee on Public Sector Responsibilities issued recommendations for further regional reforms, recommending principles for the division of responsibilities among levels and suggesting a potential restructuring of Sweden's regional map.

Sweden's approach demonstrates how iterative evaluation and feedback loops can be used to gradually refine and expand regional governance models.

Sources: McCallion, M. and P. Tallberg (2008[41]), "Regionalisation in Sweden", https://www.stals.santannapisa.it/sites/default/files/stals_Tallberg.pdf; OECD (2017[42]), *Multi-level Governance Reforms: Overview of OECD Country Experiences*, http://dx.doi.org/10.1787/9789264272866-en.

The "learning by monitoring" approach can extend to funding. For example, consider a scenario where the Estonian Government empowers the regions to execute their own regional development projects by systematically delivering additional national or EU funds through the regions, an idea that came up repeatedly among pilot regional council members and was alluded to in the draft Central Estonian agreement (OECD, 2024[36]; Central Estonian Pilot Regional Council, 2024[9]). Participating ministries might balk at contributing substantial funds, given the limited capacity of local authorities to plan, execute and invest (see Chapter 2). In this case, the Estonian Government could start by creating a small, time-limited pilot fund, pooling money from involved ministries and testing this arrangement before introducing a larger or longer-lasting arrangement. For example, it could ask relevant ministries to contribute to a fund that the pilot regional councils would administer to implement the agreements. Importantly, an impact evaluation plan should be prepared before the pilot begins. After one funding cycle, an evaluation could be carried out by an external, impartial body to ensure credibility. Based on this assessment, if the results of that exercise show that the councils managed the funds appropriately and with the desired impacts, the ministries could scale up by providing a larger pool of funds or a longer spending horizon. This incremental process – with funding ramping up incrementally as regions show signs of readiness – would allow local authorities to build capacity while the national government builds confidence in the ability of municipalities to handle additional funds.

Summary of recommendations

To capture lessons learned from the pilot regional councils and inform decisions about scaling them up, Estonia can:

1. **Evaluate whether the experiment met the Estonian Government's expectations** by linking the motivations and objectives behind the pilot regional councils to the results that they achieved. The evaluation can draw upon both qualitative and quantitative information to create a well-rounded picture of the performance and impact of each of the councils. Ultimately, this evaluation will help the Ministry of Regional Affairs and Agriculture to make decisions about their future.
2. **Involve stakeholders in the evaluation of the pilots** by soliciting their views, e.g. through a survey or interviews. Pilot regional council members are an important target of this recommendation, but the Ministry of Regional Affairs and Agriculture can also seek the perspectives of those without direct representation e.g. local authorities and ministries, who, while not sitting on the councils themselves, were engaged in the work of preparing the agreements.

To allow regional governance in Estonia to continue to develop in response to the needs of all parties and to the ability of parties to make the most of regional governance, Estonia can:

3. **Consider a phased approach to scaling up the pilots**, introducing new elements in a limited way to see how they work, and to gradually build the capacity and confidence of participants before committing to a larger-scale rollout.

Conclusion

The pilot regional councils promise to begin to lay the foundations for place-based policy for regional development in Estonia by promoting a cross-cutting approach across the government and place sensitivity to regional needs and opportunities. First, the pilot councils provide a structure that brings line ministries together to exchange on multi-dimensional regional development challenges, which can help to address a lack of systematic co-ordination for regional development across government. Second, the pilot regional councils offer a platform for exchange between the two levels of government (and with other important regional development actors), helping to address a disconnect in vertical co-ordination that restricts bottom-up input from shaping national strategy and policy. In short, Estonia's pilot regional councils represent a step towards laying the foundations for place-based policy presented in Chapter 2.

The question is whether the pilot regional councils deliver in practice, however, and the moment is right for the Estonian Government to evaluate its pilots to see how they lived up to ambitions. To start its evaluation, the Estonian Government can look back to its original rationale for the councils, to see if and how they have created new economies of scale, fostered engagement between levels of government and involved stakeholders to promote regional competitiveness. This evaluation will determine whether they show sufficient promise to justify scaling them up and provide valuable information about adjustments that should be made before they are scaled up.

The next question – which is beyond the scope of this report – will be *how* to scale up. Parties to the agreements have already expressed interest in scaling up the pilot regional councils. They have voiced interest in expanding geographically, with new regional councils to cover the other parts of Estonia. There has also been discussion of expanding regional governance by, for example, introducing regional development agencies to help with the implementation of agreements. The results of the evaluation will certainly help inform the decision of how to scale up the councils. At the same time, the Estonian Government can benefit from embracing an experimental approach again by rolling out new regional governance features in an iterative way.

References

Allain-Dupré, D. (2018), "Assigning responsibilities across levels of government: Trends, challenges and guidelines for policy-makers", *OECD Working Papers on Fiscal Federalism*, No. 24, OECD Publishing, Paris, https://doi.org/10.1787/f0944eae-en. [5]

Arenguseire Keskus (2017), "Spatial and strategic planning of development, including regional level functions in directing spatial development (rengu ruumiline ja strateegiline kavandamine, sh regionaaltasandi funktsioonid ruumilise arengu suunamisel)", https://www.etag.ee/wp-content/uploads/2018/04/Arengu-ruumiline-ja-strateegiline-kavandamine_ARUANNE_2018-02-25_RaM.pdf (accessed on 18 March 2025). [12]

Central and South Estonian Pilot Regional Councils (2024), "Draft regional development agreements", https://www.agri.ee/regionaalareng-uhistransport/regionaalareng-ja-poliitika/regionaalsed-arengulepped. [25]

Central Estonian Pilot Regional Council (2024), "Draft regional development agreement", Unpublished. [9]

Charbit, C. (2025), "Slides: State-Regions Contracts to support administrative reforms and regional development", OECD Webinar on State-Regions Contracts - 11 April 2025. [28]

Charbit, C. (2024), "The use of contracts across levels of government", Unpublished. [37]

Charbit, C. and O. Romano (2017), "Governing together: An international review of contracts across levels of government for regional development", *OECD Regional Development Working Papers*, No. 2017/04, OECD Publishing, Paris, https://doi.org/10.1787/ff7c8ac4-en. [27]

Durand, A. and M. Vincent (forthcoming), "The ABCDs of policy experimentation", *OECD Working Paper*, OECD Publishing, Paris. [38]

Estonian Government (2023), *Pilot Project on Regional Development Plans and Councils*. [14]

Estonian Ministry of Finance (2017), "The government sent the county government reform bill to the Riigikogu", https://fin.ee/uudised/valitsus-saatis-maavalitsuste-reformi-seaduseelnou-riigikokku (accessed on 2 June 2025). [44]

Estonian Ministry of Public Administration (2023), *Ministerial Decree on the Establishment of the Kesk-Eesti Regional Council (Ministri käskkiri Kesk-Eesti regionaalse arenguleppe nõukogu moodustamine)*. [18]

Estonian Ministry of Public Administration (2023), *Ministerial Decree on the Establishment of the Lõuna-Eesti Regional Council (Ministri käskkiri Lõuna-Eesti regionaalse nõukogu moodustamine)*, https://www.agri.ee/sites/default/files/documents/2024-08/arengulepe-le-nk-kk-2023-45-moodustamine.pdf. [17]

Estonian Ministry of Regional Affairs and Agriculture (2025), *Regional Development Agreements (Regionaalsed arengulepped)*, https://www.agri.ee/regionaalareng-planeeringud/kohalikud-omavalitsused/regionaalsed-arengulepped. [1]

Estonian Ministry of Regional Affairs and Agriculture (2024), "Meeting minutes of the South Estonia Development Council, 2 December 2024", https://www.agri.ee/regionaalareng-planeeringud/kohalikud-omavalitsused/regionaalsed-arengulepped (accessed on 7 March 2025). [24]

Estonian Ministry of Regional Affairs and Agriculture (2024), "Meeting minutes of the South Estonian Regional Council, 20 September 2024", https://www.agri.ee/regionaalareng-planeeringud/kohalikud-omavalitsused/regionaalsed-arengulepped#louna-eesti-arengule--2 (accessed on 7 March 2025). [26]

Estonian Ministry of Regional Affairs and Agriculture (2023), "Meeting minutes of the South Estonia Regional Council, 22 February 2023", https://www.agri.ee/regionaalareng-planeeringud/kohalikud-omavalitsused/regionaalsed-arengulepped (accessed on 7 March 2025). [22]

Etzkowitz, H. (2008), *The Triple Helix: University-Industry-Government Innovation in Action*, https://doi.org/10.4324/9780203929605. [16]

European Leader Association for Rural Development (2025), *About LEADER and CLLD*, https://elard.eu/leader-clld/. [19]

Eurostat (n.d.), *Overview: Nomenclature of Territorial Units for Statistics*, https://ec.europa.eu/eurostat/web/nuts. [7]

Iceland Ministry of Infrastructure (2023), "Interview with the OECD", OECD, Paris. [20]

Icelandic Government Steering Group on Regional Affairs (2020), *Sóknaráætlanir landshluta*, https://www.stjornarradid.is/verkefni/fleiri-rit/rit/2020/11/23/Greinargerd-um-soknaraaetlanir-landshluta-2015-2019/. [21]

Kattai, K. et al. (2020), *Analysis of Estonian Regional Development: Proposals for Shaping Regional Governance Models – Final Report (Eesti regionaaltasandi arengu analüüs: Regionaalse valitsemise mudelite kujundamise ettepanekud – Lõpparuanne)*, https://skytte.ut.ee/sites/default/files/2022-05/1.%20Regionaalne%20valitsemine%20lopparuanne_final.pdf. [3]

McCallion, M. and P. Tallberg (2008), "Regionalisation in Sweden", *STALS Research Paper*, No. 6/2008, https://www.stals.santannapisa.it/sites/default/files/stals_Tallberg.pdf. [41]

Michels, J. and Y. Wu (forthcoming), "Strengthening the impact of regional development strategies in the face of global challenges: A focus on Implementation". [35]

OECD (2024), "Information gathering interviews", OECD, Paris. [36]

OECD (2024), "Stakeholder interviews", OECD, Paris. [11]

OECD (2023), "Foresight and vision-setting workshops", OECD, Paris. [34]

OECD (2023), *Recommendation of the Council on Regional Development Policy*, OECD, Paris, https://legalinstruments.oecd.org/en/instruments/OECD-LEGAL-0492. [30]

OECD (2022), *Regional Governance in OECD Countries: Trends, Typology and Tools*, OECD Multi-level Governance Studies, OECD Publishing, Paris, https://doi.org/10.1787/4d7c6483-en. [33]

OECD (2022), *Shrinking Smartly in Estonia: Preparing Regions for Demographic Change*, OECD Rural Studies, OECD Publishing, Paris, https://doi.org/10.1787/77cfe25e-en. [4]

OECD (2022), *SNGWOFI - Iceland profile*, https://www.sng-wofi.org/country_profiles/iceland.html. [8]

OECD (2020), *Regulatory Impact Assessment*, OECD Best Practice Principles for Regulatory Policy, OECD Publishing, Paris, https://doi.org/10.1787/7a9638cb-en. [40]

OECD (2020), *The Future of Regional Development and Public Investment in Wales, United Kingdom*, OECD Multi-level Governance Studies, OECD Publishing, Paris, https://doi.org/10.1787/e6f5201d-en. [6]

OECD (2019), *Effective Public Investment Across Levels of Government: Implementing the OECD Principles*, OECD, Paris, https://www.oecd.org/en/about/projects/effective-public-investment-toolkit.html. [15]

OECD (2018), *Rethinking Regional Development Policy-making*, OECD Multi-level Governance Studies, OECD Publishing, Paris, https://doi.org/10.1787/9789264293014-en. [32]

OECD (2017), *Multi-level Governance Reforms: Overview of OECD Country Experiences*, OECD Multi-level Governance Studies, OECD Publishing, Paris, https://doi.org/10.1787/9789264272866-en. [42]

OECD (2011), *Estonia: Towards a Single Government Approach*, OECD Public Governance Reviews, OECD Publishing, Paris, https://doi.org/10.1787/9789264104860-en. [13]

OECD (2008), *Introductory Handbook for Undertaking Regulatory Impact Analysis (RIA)*, OECD, Paris, https://www.oecd.org/gov/regulatory-policy/44789472.pdf. [39]

OECD (2007), *Linking Regions and Central Governments: Contracts for Regional Development*, OECD Multi-level Governance Studies, OECD Publishing, Paris, https://doi.org/10.1787/9789264008755-en. [23]

OECD (forthcoming), *Place-Based Policies for the Future*, OECD Publishing, Paris. [31]

Riigi Teataja (2002), *Local Government Associations Act*, https://www.riigiteataja.ee/en/eli/506112013002/consolide. [2]

South Estonian Pilot Regional Council (2024), “Draft regional development agreement”, Unpublished. [10]

South Estonian Pilot Regional Council (2024), *Draft regional development agreement*, https://www.agri.ee/regionaalareng-planeeringud/kohalikud-omavalitsused/regionaalsed-arengulepped#dokumendid-ja-viited (accessed on 7 March 2025). [29]

Statistics Estonia (2021), “Levels of Administrative Units and Spatial Data”, https://rahvaloendus.ee/en/census-2021/methodology-and-quality/levels-of-administrative-units-and-spatial-data. [43]

Notes

[1] Estonia's two pilot regions differ slightly from its statistical regions. In Estonia, there are five small (NUTS 3) regions under the Nomenclature of Territorial Units for Statistics system: Central Estonia, North Estonia, Northeast Estonia, West Estonia and South Estonia (Statistics Estonia, 2021[43]). For the pilot regions, one county switched regions: the county of Viljandi requested to be included in Central Estonia instead of South Estonia.

[2] It is important to note that regional governance is not the only way to achieve economies of scale (others include inter-municipal co-operation, outsourcing or centralisation). Indeed, in some cases, it may be more effective to let municipalities collaborate flexibly on a case-by-case basis, because a fixed regional body risks imposing a one-size-fits-all approach, which may not lead to efficient service provision.

[3] A decision justified as a measure to make more efficient and rational the division of tasks among government bodies, in light of the dwindling responsibilities of county governments (Estonian Ministry of Finance, 2017[44]).

[4] The representatives of which were both transferred to a new Ministry of Regional Affairs and Agriculture with a reorganisation in the government.

[5] One way to reduce the risk of "shopping list" agreements is to anchor regional development agreements in a clearly defined national strategy for regional development (Charbit and Romano, 2017[27]). In countries where such strategies are in place (for example, Poland), contracts are typically limited to activities that contribute to both national and regional priorities.

[6] The relevant ministry (first the Ministry of Finance, then the Ministry of Regional Affairs and Agriculture) appointed a project manager from the Local Government Policy Department for each pilot regional council and an assistant project manager from the Regional Development Department. The project managers provide technical and logistical support for procedures like consultations, publicity and communications with ministries and other partners. EUR 30 000 was earmarked for 2023 for each pilot project, funding the drafting of a development agreement to external experts, the provision of expert advice and operational support for meetings (such as room hire, catering, technical services, interpretation services).

Annex A. Project methodology

This synthesis report weaves together the results of OECD activities conducted as part of the Strengthening Regional Specialisation and Competitiveness in Estonia project funded by the European Union. During this 28-month project, the OECD accompanied the Estonian Government as it tested a new approach to regional development planning and implementation. This methodological annex outlines the activities upon which this synthesis report is based, including foresight and vision-setting workshops, capacity-building workshops and action plan workshops.

- **Fact finding interviews**: The project included fact-finding interviews with over 40 representatives from central and local governments, the private sector, civil society and educational institutions.
- **Foresight and vision setting workshops**: In both Central and South Estonia, foresight workshops invited regional stakeholders – pilot regional council members, municipal and county development actors, industry representatives and others – to explore potential futures for their regions. Participants worked with facilitators to clarify their preferences for the region's future and to identify key directions for the regional development agreements. Approximately 50 participants attended across both regions.
- Follow-up vision-setting workshops in both regions (with 44 participants total) brought together representatives from national ministries, local governments, academia and civil society. These sessions guided participants through a process of solidifying their ambitions for their regions, and defining the conditions required to realise those ambitions, such as the availability of skilled labour, sufficient housing, enhanced connectivity and stronger innovation ecosystems.
- **Capacity-building workshops**: The OECD offered a capacity-building workshop on regional development contracts for the members of the two pilot regional councils. A second high-level workshop brought together vice-chancellors and senior civil servants from seven Estonian ministries to consider how to advance cross-government working for regional development.
- **Action planning**: Action-planning workshops helped the two pilot regional councils develop more detailed implementation plans. Participants prioritised between previously identified development areas, formulated specific objectives, sequenced implementation steps, assigned responsibilities and anticipated risks. After these sessions, each council had a clear roadmap of how the forthcoming development agreement would underpin the delivery of priority areas. Approximately 40 participants participated in these sessions.

Annex B. Additional figures

Net internal and external migration

Figure A B.1. Net internal migration

Net number of internal migrants by TL3 region, 2017-23

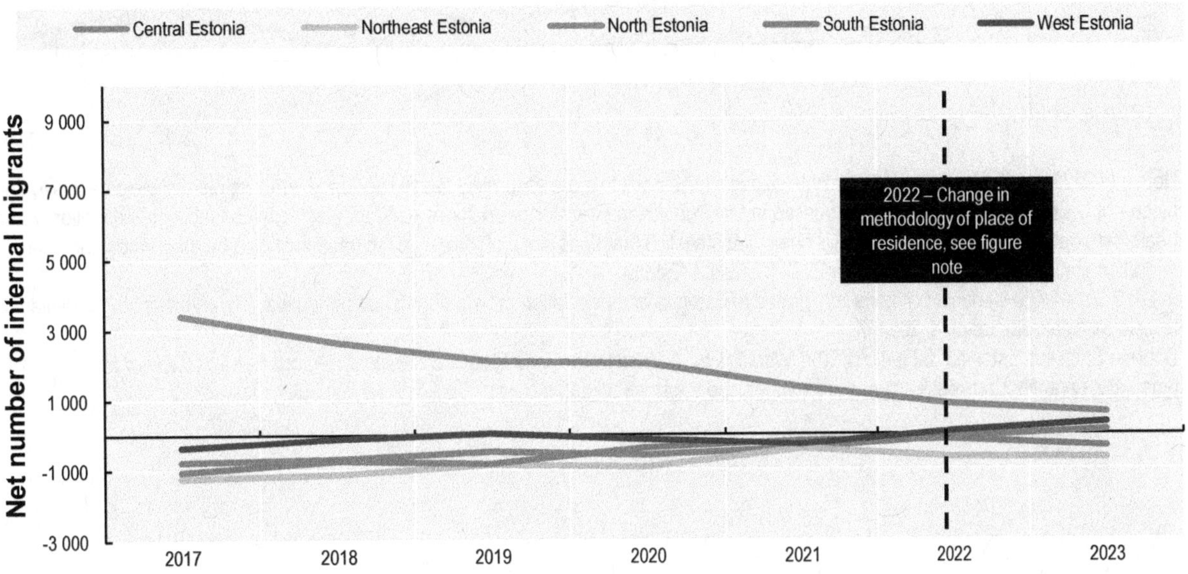

Note: In 2022, the Estonian Government introduced a new index to more accurately gauge residence, drawing on multiple datasets to determine places of residence (e.g. looking at addresses in the Population Register, property ownership, electricity connections, education information, healthcare data, etc.). Internal migration is one of the statistics that uses place of residence, so caution should be used when comparing internal migration statistics from before and after 2022 (Statistics Estonia, 2022[1]).
Source: Statistics Estonia (2023[2]), *RVR02: Migration by Administrative Unit/Type of Settlement Region, Sex and Type of Migration*, https://andmed.stat.ee/en/stat/rahvastik__rahvastikusundmused__ranne/RVR02.

Figure A B.2. Net external migration

Net number of external migrants by TL3 region, 2017-23

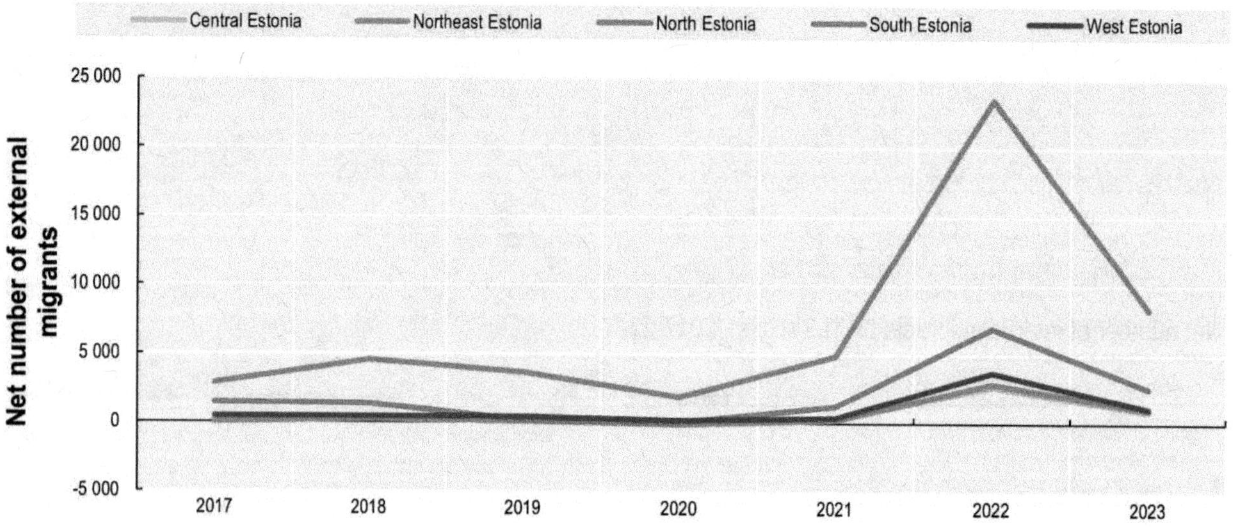

Notes: In 2022, the Estonian Government introduced a new index to more accurately gauge residence, drawing on multiple datasets to determine places of residence (e.g. looking at addresses in the Population Register, property ownership, electricity connections, education information, healthcare data, etc.). Internal migration is one of the statistics that uses place of residence, so caution should be used when comparing internal migration statistics from before and after 2022 (Statistics Estonia, 2022[1]).
In 2022-23, 44 480 Ukrainian citizens immigrated to Estonia, and population growth during that period was driven mostly by Ukrainians arriving in Estonia (Statistics Estonia, 2024[3]).
Source: Statistics Estonia (2023[2]), *RVR02: Migration by Administrative Unit/Type of Settlement Region, Sex and Type of Migration*, https://andmed.stat.ee/en/stat/rahvastik__rahvastikusundmused__ranne/RVR02.

Value added by region, sector and subsector

Figure A B.3. Value-added by region and sector

Shares of value-added from agriculture, forestry and fishing, industry and construction, and services by TL3 region, 2023

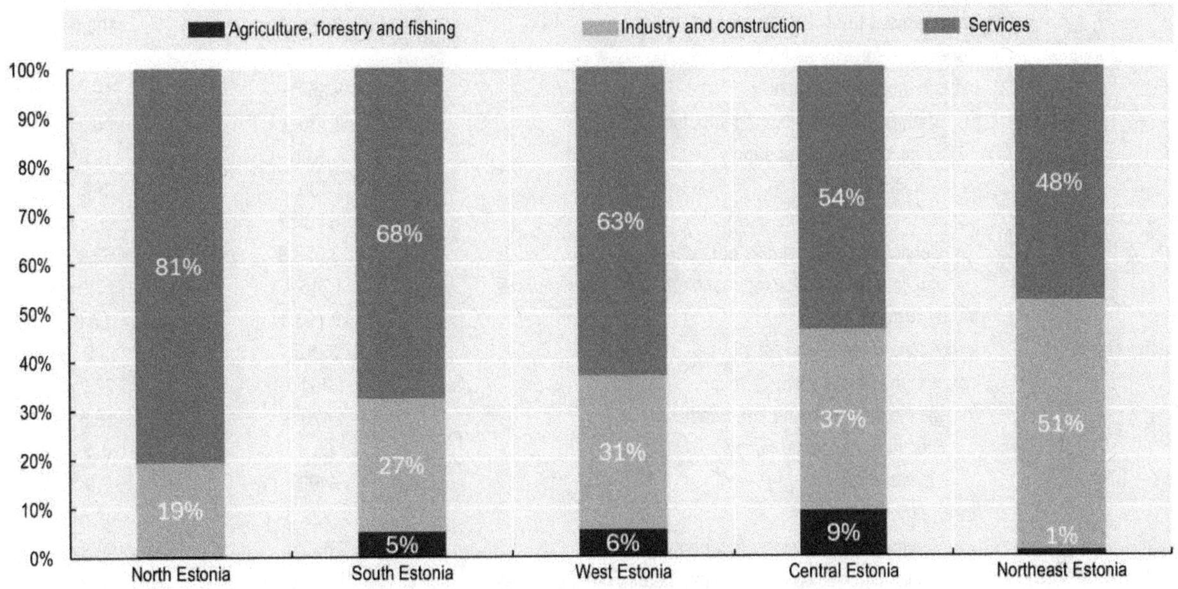

Notes: Services include: wholesale and retail trade, repair of motor vehicles and motorcycles; transportation and storage; accommodation and food service activities; information and communication; financial and insurance activities; real estate activities; professional, scientific and technical activities; administrative and support service activities; public administration and defence, compulsory social security; education; human health and social work activities; arts, entertainment and recreation; other service activities; households as employers and other activities. Industry and construction include: mining and quarrying; manufacturing; electricity, gas, steam and air conditioning supply; water supply; sewerage, waste management and remediation activities; construction.
Source: Statistics Estonia (Statistics Estonia, 2023[4]), RAA0051: Gross Domestic Product by County and Economic Sector T (ESA 2010), https://andmed.stat.ee/en/stat/majandus__rahvamajanduse-arvepidamine__sisemajanduse-koguprodukt-(skp)__regionaalne-sisemajanduse-koguprodukt/RAA0051/table/tableViewLayout2.

Table A B.1. Value-added by region, sector, and subsector, 2023

		Value at current prices (EUR million)	Share of economic activity in region's value-added (%)
Central Estonia	Agriculture, forestry and fishing	184.2	9.4
	Industry and construction	720.5	36.8
	Mining and quarrying; manufacturing	536.0	27.4
	Electricity and water supply	18.7	1.0
	Construction	165.8	8.5
	Services	1 052.9	53.8
	Services of the business economy	702.5	35.9
	Public administration, education, health; other services	350.4	17.9
	Value-added total	**1 957.6**	**100.0**
Northeast Estonia	Agriculture, forestry and fishing	28.1	1.2
	Industry and construction	1 174.8	50.9
	Mining and quarrying; manufacturing	433.8	18.8

		Value at current prices (EUR million)	Share of economic activity in region's value-added (%)
	Electricity and water supply	661.9	28.7
	Construction	79.1	3.4
	Services	1 103.7	47.8
	Services of the business economy	714.0	31.0
	Public administration, education, health; other services	389.7	16.9
	Value-added total	**2 306.6**	**100.0**
North Estonia	Agriculture, forestry and fishing	66.4	0.3
	Industry and construction	3 959.5	19.0
	Mining and quarrying; manufacturing	2 130.9	10.2
	Electricity and water supply	638.5	3.1
	Construction	1 190.1	5.7
	Services	16 769.2	80.6
	Services of the business economy	13 053.8	62.8
	Public administration, education, health; other services	3 715.4	17.9
	Value-added total	**20 795.1**	**100.0**
South Estonia	Agriculture, forestry and fishing	325.3	5.2
	Industry and construction	1 704.7	27.2
	Mining and quarrying; manufacturing	1 178.9	18.8
	Electricity and water supply	85.4	1.4
	Construction	440.5	7.0
	Services	4 227.3	67.6
	Services of the business economy	2 552.4	40.8
	Public administration, education, health; other services	1 675.0	26.8
	Value-added total	**6 257.3**	**100.0**
West Estonia	Agriculture, forestry and fishing	131.8	5.6
	Industry and construction	743.3	31.4
	Mining and quarrying; manufacturing	469.2	19.8
	Electricity and water supply	44.5	1.9
	Construction	229.6	9.7
	Services	1 493.5	63.1
	Services of the business economy	1 023.4	43.2
	Public administration, education, health; other services	470.1	19.8
	Value-added total	**2 368.6**	**100.0**
Whole country	Agriculture, forestry and fishing	735.8	2.2
	Industry and construction	8 302.8	24.6
	Mining and quarrying; manufacturing	4 748.8	14.1
	Electricity and water supply	1 449.0	4.3
	Construction	2 105.0	6.2
	Services	24 646.6	73.2
	Services of the business economy	18 046.1	53.6
	Public administration, education, health; other services	6 600.5	19.6
	Value-added total	**33 685.2**	**100.0**

Notes: "Electricity and water supply" refers to: electricity, gas, steam and air conditioning supply; water supply; sewerage, waste management and remediation activities.
"Services of the business economy" refers to: wholesale and retail trade; repair of motor vehicles and motorcycles; transportation and storage; accommodation and food service activities; information and communication; financial and insurance activities; real estate activities; professional, scientific and technical activities; administrative and support service activities.
"Public administration, education, health; other services" refers to: public administration and defence; compulsory social security; education; human health and social work activities; arts, entertainment and recreation; other service activities; households as employers and other activities.
Source: Statistics Estonia (2023[5]), *RAA0052: Gross Domestic Product by Region and Economic Activity (ESA 2010)*, https://andmed.stat.ee/en/stat/majandus__rahvamajanduse-arvepidamine__sisemajanduse-koguprodukt-(skp)__regionaalne-sisemajanduse-koguprodukt/RAA0052/table/tableViewLayout2.

Labour productivity by main economic activity

Figure A B.4. Labour productivity in agriculture, forestry and fishing, 2013-22

USD per worker, PPP converted, units, constant prices (2020)

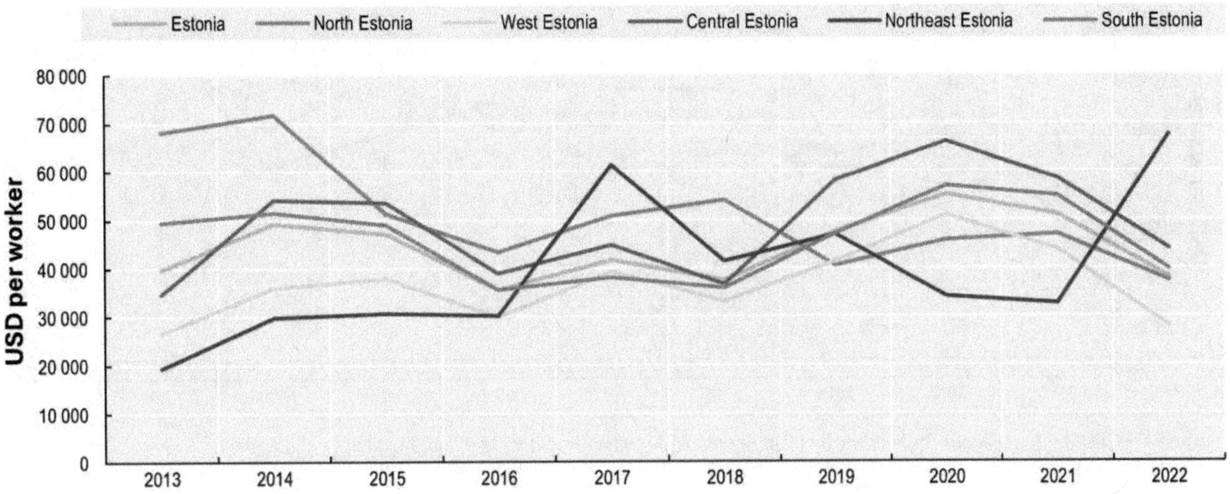

Source: OECD (2022[6]), *Labour Productivity by Main Economic Activity – Regions*, http://data-explorer.oecd.org/s/1yx.

Figure A B.5. Labour productivity in industry (except construction), 2013-22

USD per worker, PPP converted, units, constant prices (2020)

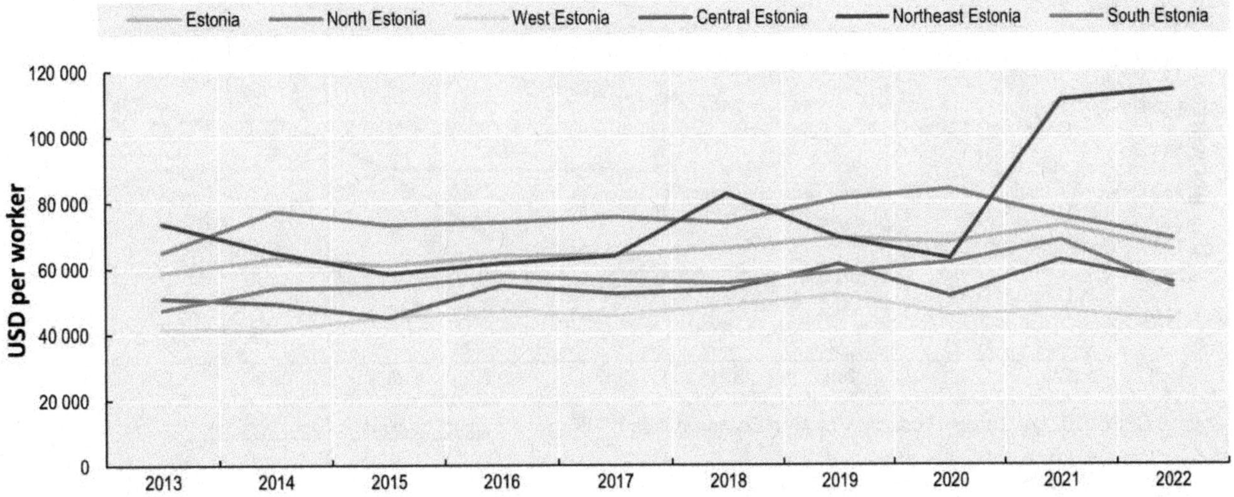

Source: OECD (2022[6]), *Labour Productivity by Main Economic Activity – Regions*, http://data-explorer.oecd.org/s/1yx.

Figure A B.6. Labour productivity in manufacturing, 2013-22

USD per worker, PPP converted, units, constant prices (2020)

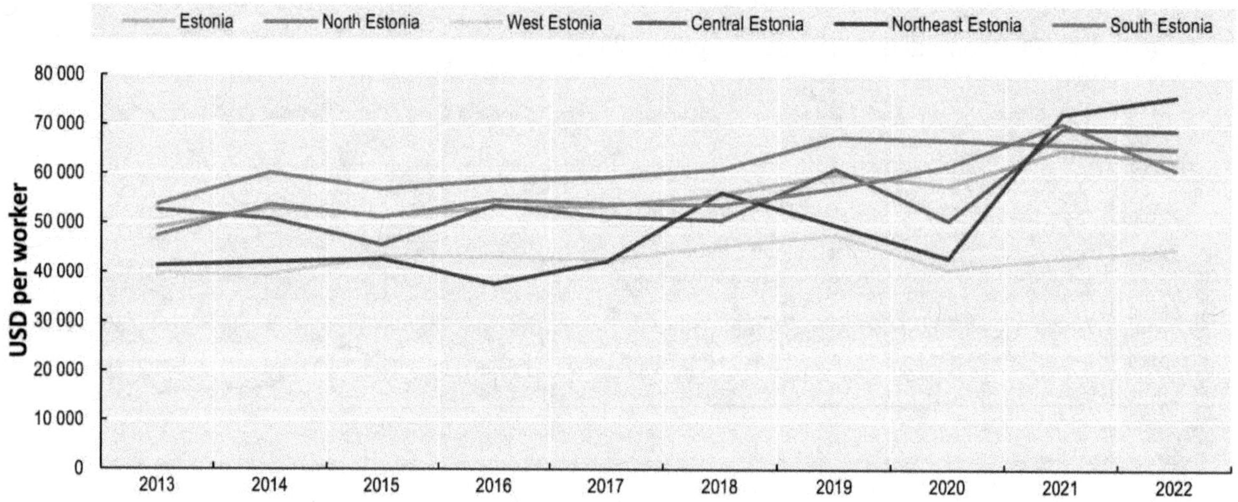

Source: OECD (2022[6]), *Labour Productivity by Main Economic Activity – Regions*, http://data-explorer.oecd.org/s/1yx.

Figure A B.7. Labour productivity in construction, 2013-22

USD per worker, PPP converted, units, constant prices (2020)

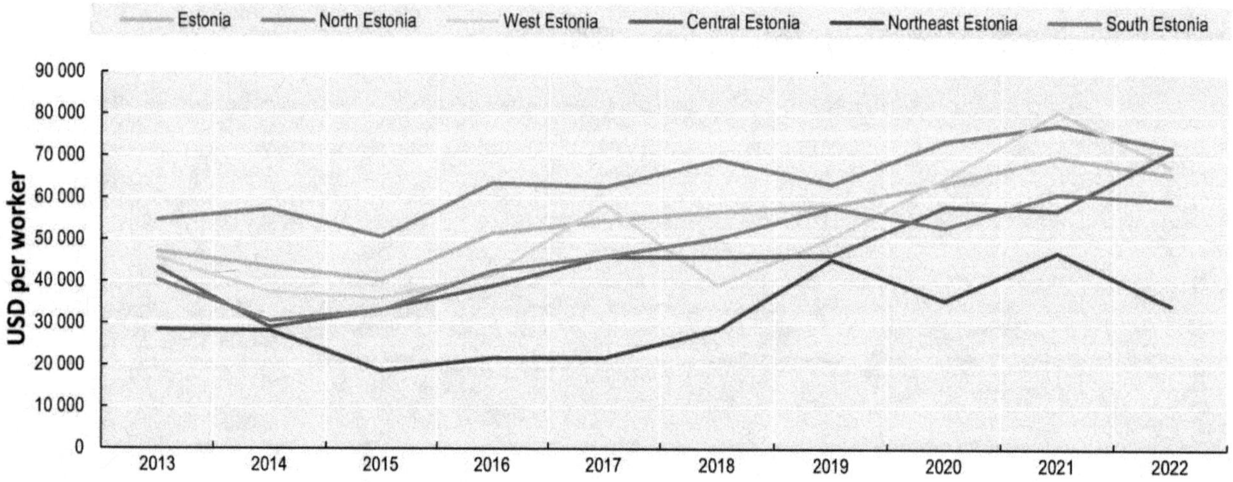

Source: OECD (2022[6]), *Labour Productivity by Main Economic Activity – Regions*, http://data-explorer.oecd.org/s/1yx.

Figure A B.8. Labour productivity in wholesale and retail trade, repair of motor vehicles and motorcycles, transportation and storage, accommodation and food service activities, 2013-22

USD per worker, PPP converted, units, constant prices (2020)

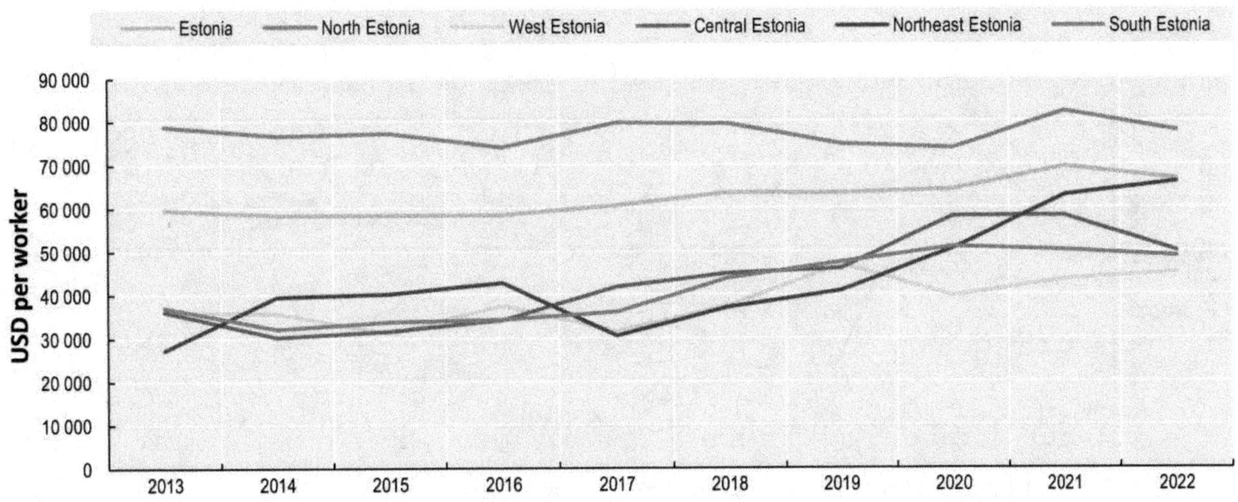

Source: OECD (2022[6]), *Labour Productivity by Main Economic Activity – Regions*, http://data-explorer.oecd.org/s/1yx.

Figure A B.9. Labour productivity in information and communication, 2013-22

USD per worker, PPP converted, units, constant prices (2020)

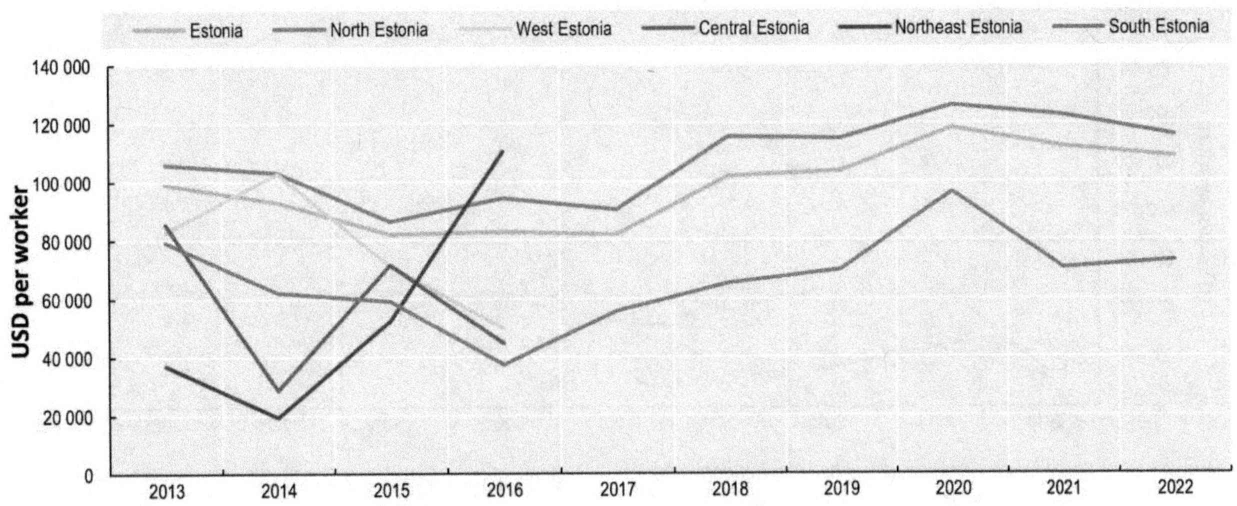

Source: OECD (2022[6]), *Labour Productivity by Main Economic Activity – Regions*, http://data-explorer.oecd.org/s/1yx.

Figure A B.10. Labour productivity in financial and insurance activities, 2013-22

USD per worker, PPP converted, units, constant prices (2020)

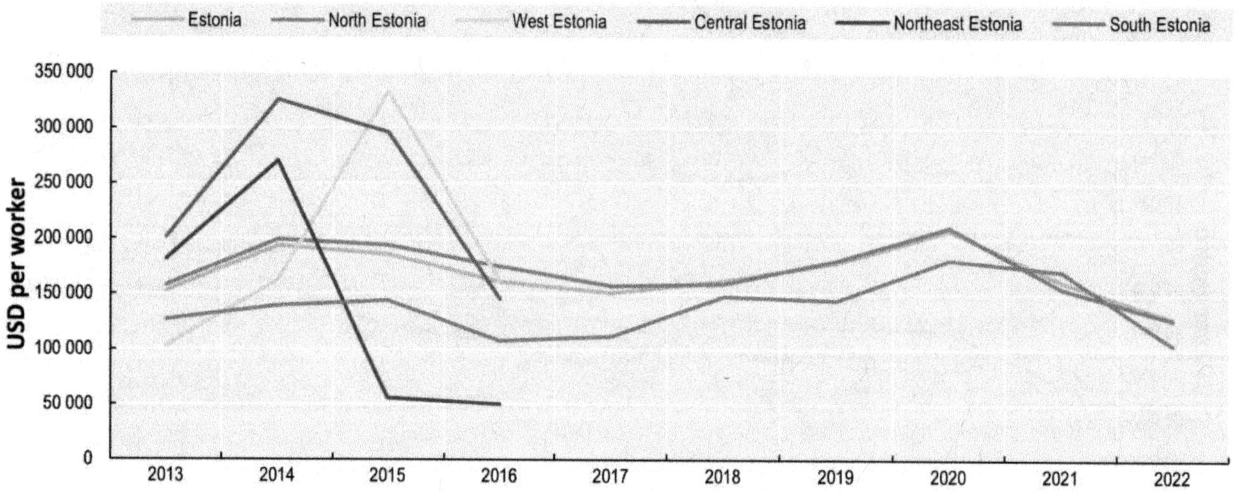

Source: OECD (2022[6]), *Labour Productivity by Main Economic Activity – Regions*, http://data-explorer.oecd.org/s/1yx.

Figure A B.11. Labour productivity in real estate activities, 2013-22

USD per worker, PPP converted, units, constant prices (2020)

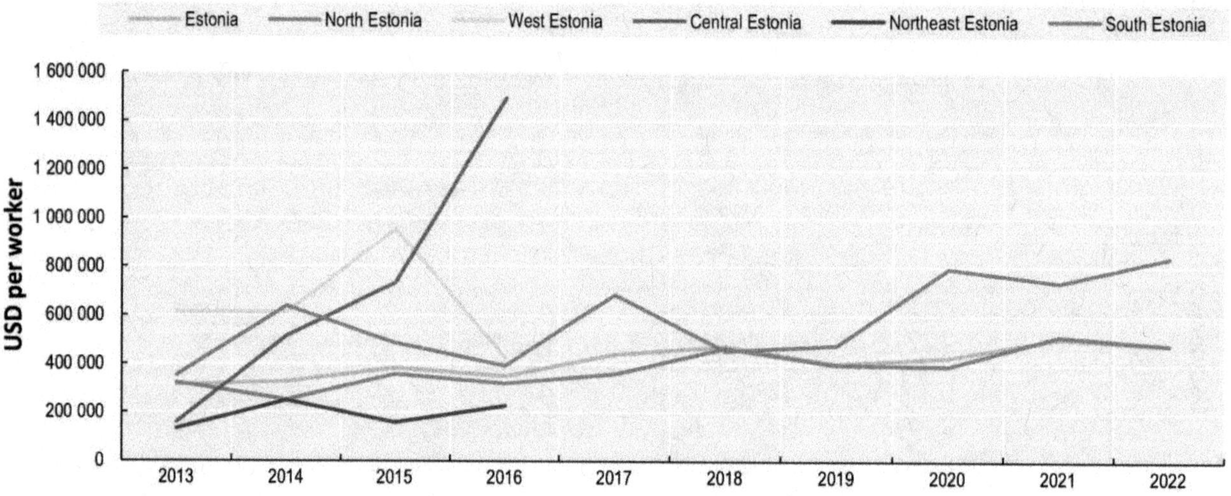

Source: OECD (2022[6]), *Labour Productivity by Main Economic Activity – Regions*, http://data-explorer.oecd.org/s/1yx.

Figure A B.12. Labour productivity in professional, scientific and technical activities, administrative and support service activities, 2013-22

USD per worker, PPP converted, units, constant prices (2020)

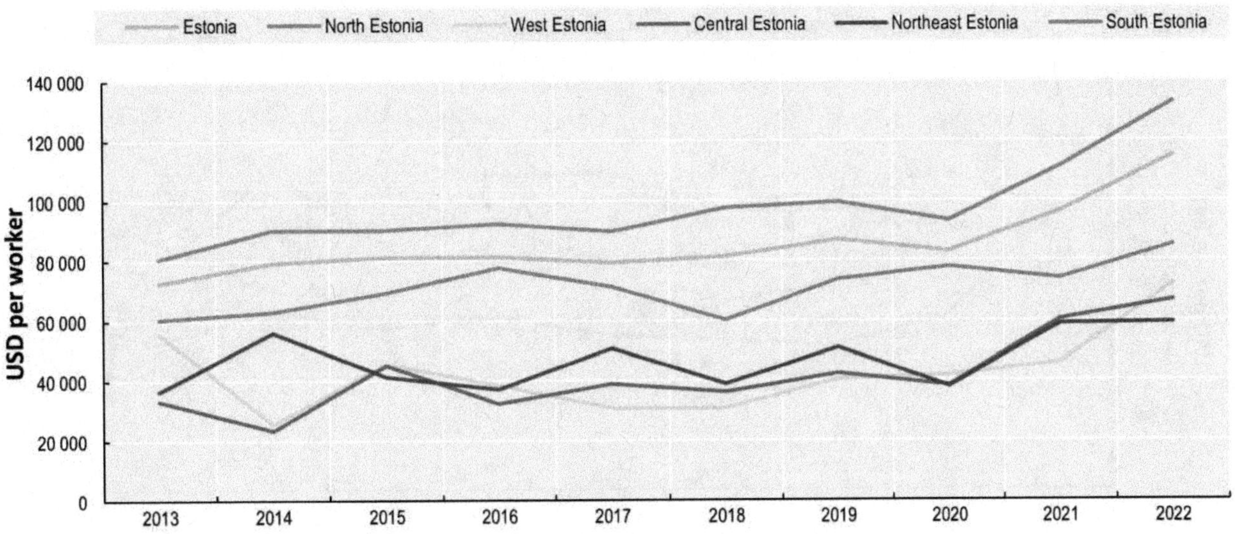

Source: OECD (2022[6]), *Labour Productivity by Main Economic Activity – Regions*, http://data-explorer.oecd.org/s/1yx.

Figure A B.13. Labour productivity in public administration, defence, education, human health and social work activities, 2013-22

USD per worker, PPP converted, units, constant prices (2020)

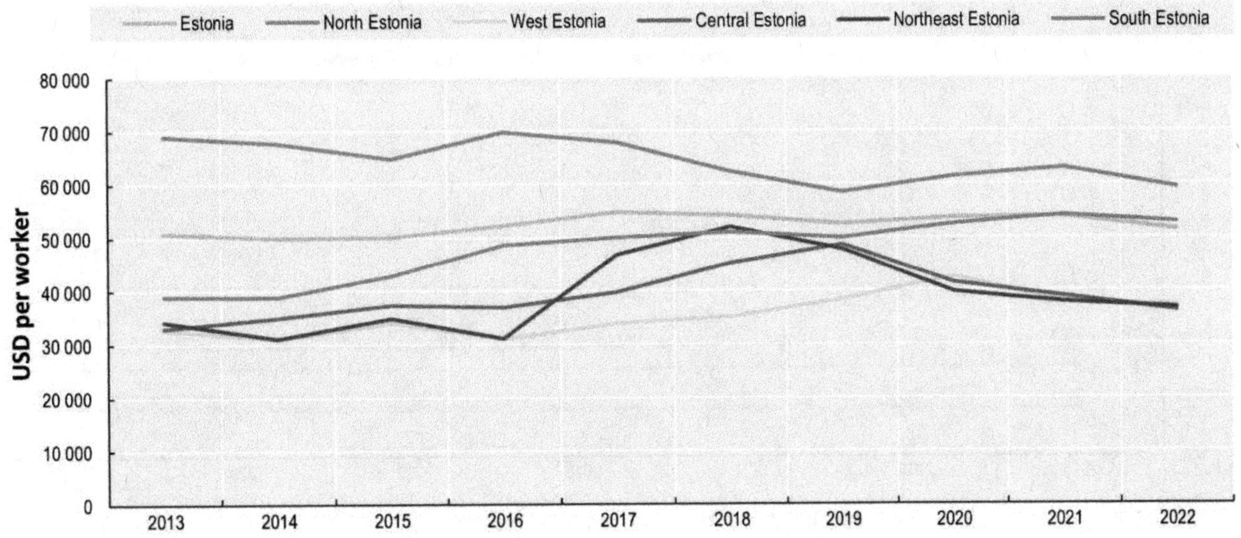

Source: OECD (2022[6]), *Labour Productivity by Main Economic Activity – Regions*, http://data-explorer.oecd.org/s/1yx.

Figure A B.14. Labour productivity in arts, entertainment and recreation, other service activities, activities of household and extraterritorial organisations and bodies, 2013-22

USD per worker, PPP converted, units, constant prices (2020)

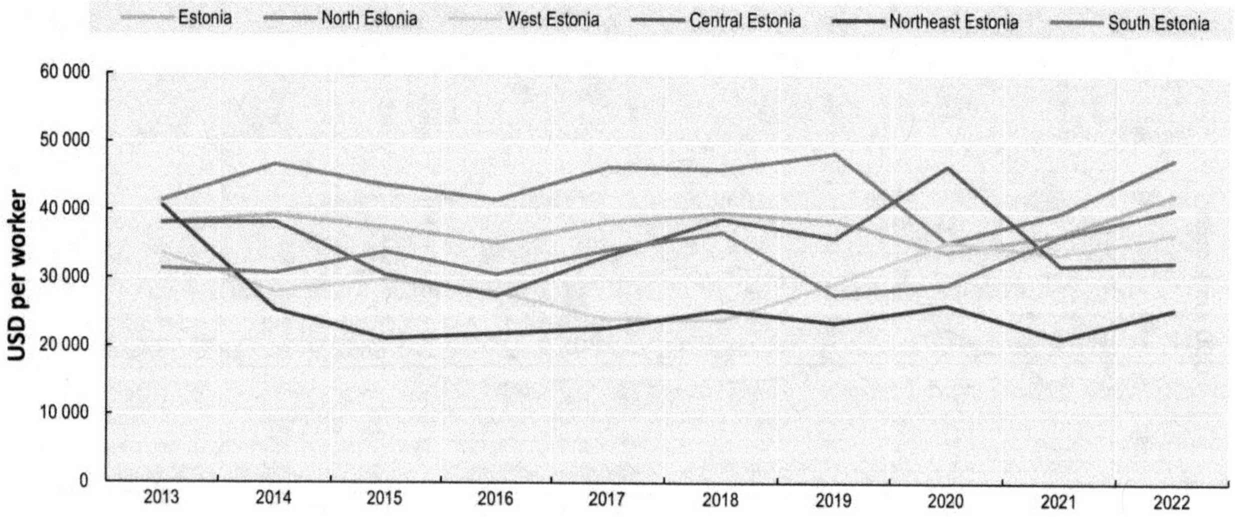

Source: OECD (2022[6]), *Labour Productivity by Main Economic Activity – Regions*, http://data-explorer.oecd.org/s/1yx.

Educational attainment by region over time

Figure A B.15. Pre-primary, primary and lower secondary educational attainment

Educational attainment by region, percentage of the population from 25 to 65 years, 2015-21

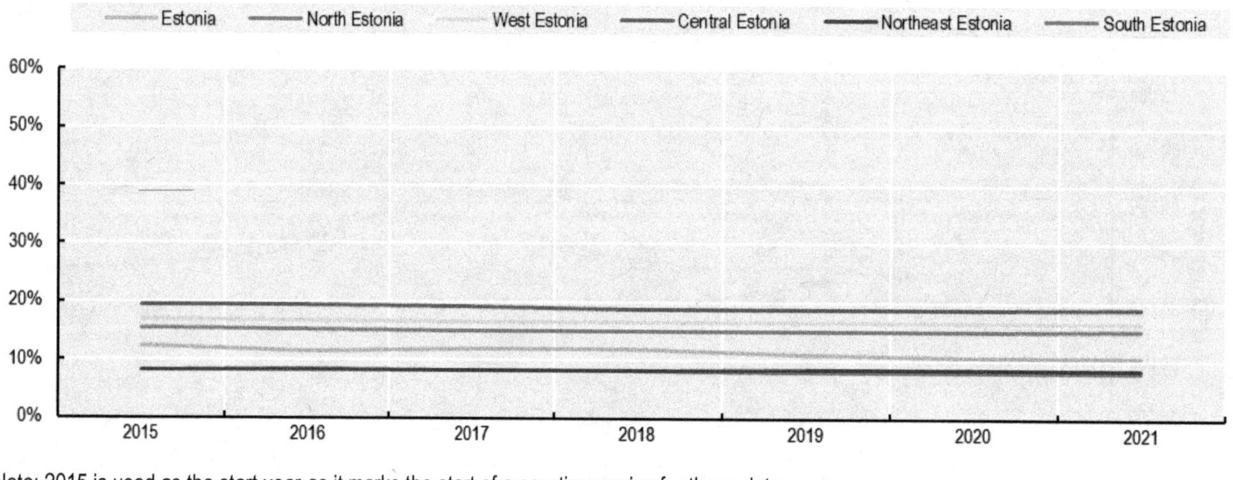

Note: 2015 is used as the start year as it marks the start of a new time series for these data.
Source: OECD (2025[7]), *Educational Attainment – Regions*, http://data-explorer.oecd.org/s/1l0.

Figure A B.16. Upper secondary and post-secondary non-tertiary educational attainment

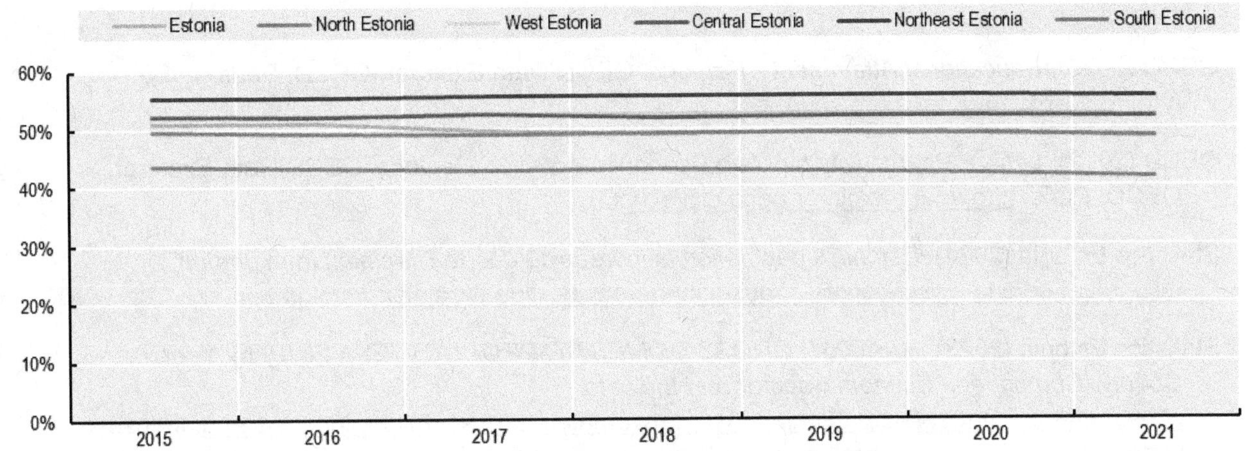

Note: 2015 is used as the start year as it marks the start of a new time series for these data.
Source: OECD (2025[7]), *Educational Attainment – Regions*, http://data-explorer.oecd.org/s/1l0.

Figure A B.17. Tertiary educational attainment

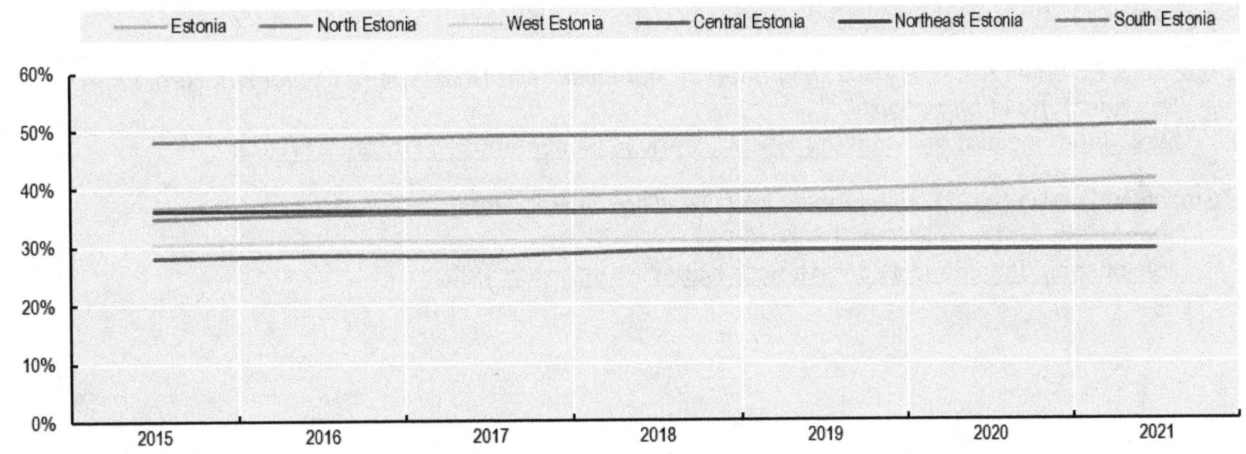

Note: 2015 is used as the start year as it marks the start of a new time series for these data.
Source: OECD (2025[7]), *Educational Attainment – Regions*, http://data-explorer.oecd.org/s/1l0.

References

OECD (2025), *Educational Attainment - Regions*, OECD Data Explorer, OECD, Paris, http://data-explorer.oecd.org/s/1l0. [7]

OECD (2022), *Labour Productivity by Main Economic Activity - Regions*, OECD Data Explorer, OECD, Paris, http://data-explorer.oecd.org/s/1yx. [6]

Statistics Estonia (2024), *Estonia's population is increasing due to Ukrainian immigration*, https://stat.ee/en/news/estonias-population-increasing-due-ukrainian-immigration. [3]

Statistics Estonia (2023), *RAA0051: GROSS DOMESTIC PRODUCT (ESA 2010) by Year, County, Component/ Economic sector and Indicator*, https://andmed.stat.ee/en/stat/majandus__rahvamajanduse-arvepidamine__sisemajanduse-koguprodukt-(skp)__regionaalne-sisemajanduse-koguprodukt/RAA0051/table/tableViewLayout2. [4]

Statistics Estonia (2023), *RAA0052: Gross Domestic Product by Region and Economic Activity (ESA 2010)*, https://andmed.stat.ee/en/stat/majandus__rahvamajanduse-arvepidamine__sisemajanduse-koguprodukt-(skp)__regionaalne-sisemajanduse-koguprodukt/RAA0052/table/tableViewLayout2. [5]

Statistics Estonia (2023), *RVR02: Migration by Administrative Unit/Type of Settlement Region, Sex and Type of Migration*, https://andmed.stat.ee/en/stat/rahvastik__rahvastikusundmused__ranne/RVR02. [2]

Statistics Estonia (2022), *Households and Dwellings in Registers*, https://www.stat.ee/sites/default/files/2022-05/Households%20and%20residences%20in%20registers.pdf. [1]

www.ingramcontent.com/pod-product-compliance
Lightning Source LLC
LaVergne TN
LVHW060453061126
851857LV00016B/1810
* 9 7 8 9 2 6 4 7 0 6 4 7 7 *